Design with TASTE

Design with
TASTE

LIZ FIREBAUGH, CKD

PUBLISHED BY
NICKEL DESIGN, INC.

Published by Nickel Design, Inc.
109 Water Street
Boyne City, Michigan 49712
info@nickeldesigninc.com

ISBN: 0-9787824-0-2

Printed in Canada.

Book Design by Nickel Design, Inc.
Art Director & Designer: Michele Nickel-Frasz
Copywriter & Editor: Gerianne Dietze

To my clients,

WHO WELCOMED ME INTO THEIR HOMES
AND INTO THEIR DREAMS.

Acknowledgements

SO MANY PEOPLE HAVE CONTRIBUTED TO THIS BOOK, I FEAR I MIGHT MISS ACKNOWLEDGING SOMEONE. THIS PROJECT HAS TAKEN WELL OVER THREE YEARS TO COME TO FRUITION, AND IT WOULD NOT HAVE BEEN POSSIBLE WITHOUT THE COMMITMENT AND ENCOURAGEMENT OF SO MANY. I AM DEEPLY GRATEFUL FOR THEIR SUPPORT.

My husband Jim, thank you for believing in me and in this book, and for embracing my passion for kitchens. You have always accepted my dedication and commitment to projects—even the really long ones. Thank you for letting destiny dictate the course of our lives.

For my daughter Taylor, you are the light in my heart and the wings of my spirit. I hope this project will encourage you to find and follow your own life's passion.

For Mom and Dad, I am so blessed to be your daughter. To Mom, who likes to listen as much as I like to talk; your calming influence sustained me throughout this long project. Dad, your steady influence has guided me throughout my life; I have always worked to make you proud. For both, your support, confidence and encouragement helped me find the spirit to follow through.

For my sisters, those great sounding boards and confidants, who took my calls and gave me their guidance no matter what time of day or night. And for my entire family who supported this project with their usual enthusiasm.

For Amy, my assistant and professional partner. Thank you for always picking up the pieces or figuring things out when I couldn't. You finish my sentences and always know what I'm thinking.

Professionally, I owe a great deal of thanks to the builders, developers, industry suppliers, and manufacturers who gave me a chance in the early years of my career. Their confidence in my ability and their willingness to take a chance have helped to shape my professional life.

For the following individuals, with gratitude:

MICHELE NICKEL-FRASZ: A creative and brilliant person who shared my passion and enthusiasm for this project. This book just begins to showcase your talent. Thank you for your encouragement and positive attitude, which had to prevail in order for this book to become a reality.

GERIANNE DIETZE: Who crafted the text so that it said what I wanted it to say. Thank you for your dedication and determination in making sure that every word had meaning.

DAN SEBOLD: Who believed in me and trusted me with his clients.

MARTIN GRABER: A man of his word.

NITA CROFF: My genuine, loyal friend and bookkeeper.

GLENDA JEHLE: My wildly enthusiastic childhood friend who knows the true meaning of friendship.

CARYN SIEGEL: A professional acquaintance who became a valued friend.

LYNDA PANARETOS: To an extraordinary person who entrusted me with her two kitchens and became a valued friend.

GREG & DENISE WHITE: For your genuine friendship and continuous encouragement and camaraderie through life's journey.

LINDA MASON: A talented design professional and friend.

HELEN LUNDSTROM: My mentor and the first to teach me about custom kitchens.

DAVID SNYDER: A professional colleague, but also a friend and confidante.

JANE VONVOIGTLANDER: For her gracious friendship and support.

JOE BLACHY: For giving me a chance.

ANNA & JORA GUT KNECHT: For testing so many recipes.

WALT BOESE: In fond memory of this special man.

Finally, I cannot forget the people whose cooperation was crucial to this book—my clients—who gave freely of their thoughts and feelings, not to mention their recipes. Thank you so very much for allowing me to work with you.

Foreword

Working with Liz, you soon find out that designing isn't just a job, but a passion.

This passion is exhibited through her enthusiasm, drive, commitment to client, and

most of all, her creativity. Liz creates one-of-a-kind design solutions that are always

on the cutting edge of style. I look forward to our continued relationship, and I

thank Liz for her commitment to Dutch Made. It is designers like Liz who have

helped make Dutch Made internationally known for handmade custom cabinetry.

I am honored to introduce this wonderful book featuring Liz's great creations.

Martin Graber

Founder & President
Dutch Made Custom Cabinetry

Contents

More than
just another room.

Amererican kitchens are many things: workrooms, assembly lines, family meeting places, and entertainment centers. The professionally designed kitchen can be all this, plus much more. It can take functionality to a new height, while presenting itself as both a showplace and a work of art. The well-designed space evokes the personality of the owner while following the dictates of good design technique. Kitchen design is a process that takes the workaday room into the loftier realm of interior design. The right kitchen looks great, works smart, and turns heads.

Putting this book to good use.

LET *Design with Taste* BECOME YOUR SOURCE FOR INSPIRATION, FOR DESIGN IDEAS, AND FOR FAVORED RECIPES.

The traditional cookbook is a how-to manual on food; this effort is a compendium of working kitchens, the people who love them, and the recipes that emanate from them.

Use this book as a reference point for style and design, and as a sourcebook for products and materials. Then sample the recipes that have been collected from these Signature Kitchens clients—delicious proof that a fabulous kitchen can really cook.

Working
WITH A KITCHEN DESIGNER

D esigners are both artists and facilitators. They guide the process and often influence the outcome, using a bank of client information to determine what is best for the job. Decisions are based not only on decorative style, but also on lifestyle, and the conscientious designer will take into account a wealth of details about the needs of the client.

Communication Arts.

THE KITCHEN DESIGNER GETS TO KNOW THE CLIENT'S NEEDS AND PREFERENCES IN MANY WAYS: THROUGH CONVERSATION, INFORMAL DRAWINGS, PICTURES TAKEN FROM MAGAZINES, OR A LIST OF WISHES AND MUST-HAVES. IT HELPS TO COMMUNICATE WELL AND OFTEN, AND IT IS THROUGH THIS PROCESS THAT DESIGN IDEAS COME TO LIFE.

Primary or Secondary?

The kitchen in the weekend getaway or cottage functions differently than the primary kitchen. Is cooking a predominant activity or an afterthought? Are weekends active or quiet? Is mealtime a family event? Does the kitchen need to accommodate simple breakfasts, cocktail parties, or large holiday gatherings? Designers can guide the client through the distinctions.

Size Matters

The size of the household has a lot to do with the dimensions of the kitchen. Active singles have their own needs; empty nesters, likewise. A growing family will want—and require—abundant space for children, friends, and school projects. Household size can dictate appliance options, walk-in pantry needs, and ultimately, the kitchen footprint.

Dinner at Eight

The typical American mealtime takes many forms: family sit-downs, or a quick bite before heading out the door, for example. Likewise, busy timetables often mean that family members eat at different times. The kitchen designer will take those eating habits into account and will anticipate future changes in family size and lifestyle.

Entertainment Center

For a casual gathering, guests typically gravitate to the kitchen. The designer will anticipate this with varied seating and traffic plans, while still allowing for the needs of the cook. Designers also know that buffets and cocktail fare require ample refrigeration, heating, and counter space. For more formal affairs, the kitchen must accommodate numerous courses and family schedules, and sometimes even a catering staff.

Parting Thoughts

Finally, the kitchen can also function as an office, a media center, a workroom for hobbies and crafts, and a showplace for collections of all kinds. Part of the designer's task is to include built-in desks or message areas with computer capabilities, hidden TV screens, extra storage for supplies, or decorative shelving and glass-fronted display cabinets based on the client's needs and taste.

Elements

OF DESIGN

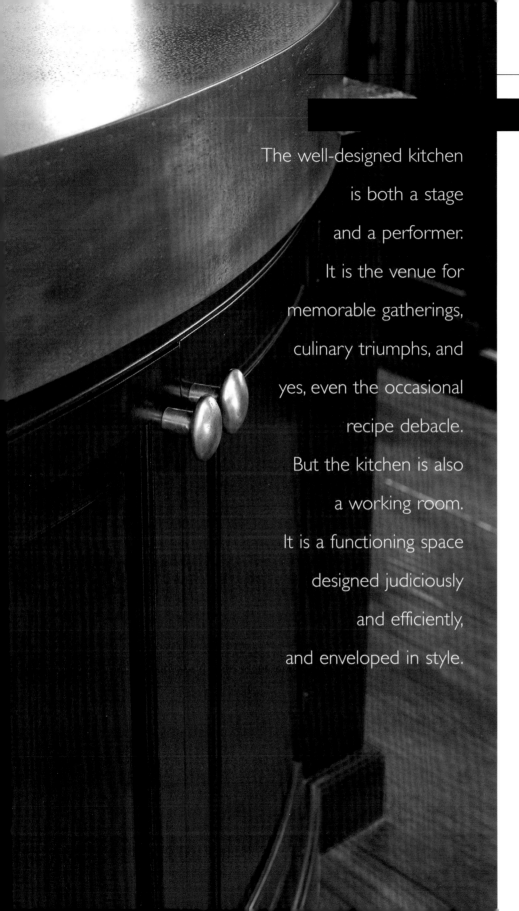

The well-designed kitchen is both a stage and a performer. It is the venue for memorable gatherings, culinary triumphs, and yes, even the occasional recipe debacle. But the kitchen is also a working room. It is a functioning space designed judiciously and efficiently, and enveloped in style.

The elements of design.

Design is both a science and an art, the combining of form and function, scale and interpretation. It is technical. It is artistic. It is referenced by the classical, the traditional, the eclectic, or the sublime. Good design follows the rules, but knows when to bend.

Likewise, the successful kitchen designer provides his or her own guidelines, but also follows those of the client. The designer loves the "putting together" of dreams and ideas while nurturing the client's vision into a practical reality.

Setting the Stage

STYLE

The first dimension of cabinetry is style—the nuanced forms that attract the eye and sometimes, even the emotions. And, since the kitchen is the busiest room in today's home, it's best to find a style that blends both taste and character. Contemporary cabinetry is a solution for someone seeking an uncluttered space driven by the unique marriage of clean lines and functionality. Sometimes Arts & Crafts, with just a hint of definition, is what catches the eye. Cottage, country, and rustic styles are full of expression, with beadboard accents, wainscot paneling, or artisan craftsmanship. But cabinets can be ornate as well, with carvings and corbels, onlays and moldings, columns and pilasters. French Provincial, Victorian, Country French, and Old English—there is a style for every taste. And, if that's not enough, mixing styles is a current trend. Cabinetry combinations can be eclectic and inspired, whimsical and irreverent. And always just right.

A Fine Finish

FINISHES

Beyond its obvious importance as storage, today's cabinetry is in keeping with the workmanship and detailing of fine furniture. Distinctive woods, native or exotic, are rubbed, carved, and coaxed to perfection. For the post-modernist, the details are in the rich grain of a fine wood, or the subtle sheen of an unexpected material such as stainless steel. A current approach calls for a generous mix of wood finishes and decorator colors. Painted cabinets—distressed, softly glazed, or finished to a high sheen—add a charge of color and work congenially with their wood counterparts. And just as colors mix, so do wood tones. It is not at all unusual for several colors and wood finishes to share space—and define task areas—in the custom kitchen. Maple and mahogany, pine and alder, for example, can easily co-exist with cream and sage, or red and blue. Cabinetry loves to put on a show.

The Storage Solution

STORAGE

The modern kitchen is an organizational wonder thanks to an industry-wide evolution in cabinetry. Yes, there are still adjustable shelves behind some of those doors, but the options have become specialized to address tasks and storage needs. Cabinets might have rollout shelves for easy access to large pots and small appliances. Pullout bins are a useful cache for recyclables. Cabinets dedicated to canned goods work extra hard with tall, two-sided pullout racks—no more blind reaching to the back of the cabinet—and smaller vertical cabinets near the cook/prep center store spices and other seasonings. Drawers, too, have benefited from this change: custom inserts eliminate the clutter of utensils or cutlery; felt-lined drawers store and protect silver; wide shallow drawers keep table linens wrinkle-free; or deep drawers with removable peg systems store dishes. Visual impact is not forgotten, however. Decorative plate racks, custom cookbook shelves, and glass-fronted display cabinets look good, but also function well for everyday use. In short, custom storage keeps the kitchen in good working order.

Working Parts

A P P L I A N C E S

White or pink? Avocado or burnt orange? Almond or stainless? We can tell the decades by the color of our appliances, but now our choices are far more diverse than color. Today's appliances have been deconstructed and reconfigured to perform their basic tasks in more convenient ways and in multiple locations. It's a strategy that makes sense and contributes to a new sense of ease in the kitchen. Streamlined components integrated into the cabinetry are key to this new way of thinking. Drawers, for example, function as refrigerators, dishwashers, freezers, and microwaves. Have one or multiples in strategic locations for prep, cooking, clean-up, and entertaining. Wine coolers, once considered extravagant, have become the must-have item in many kitchens. Newer to the American kitchen, but gaining steady ground, are built-in computerized coffee makers, ready and able to brew a single cup of coffee, espresso, or cappuccino on demand. Microwave and convection ovens can handle virtually any task on their own, or lend back-up to the European ranges that anchor the well-planned room. Cooktops, too, have evolved to serve multiple needs. Grills, woks, steamers, and combination gas/electric burners are routine features. Out of sight—but all-important—are the structural supports, venting systems, and power sources needed to accommodate these myriad appliance choices. In fact, choosing appliances and their locations is a crucial early step in kitchen planning.

The Kitchen Sink

WATERWORKS

The kitchen sink is far more than the utilitarian catch-all it once was. Basins have been restyled for function and relocated for convenience; and while the traditional double sink is still common, it is not the only choice. Small specialized sinks are strategically placed for particular jobs—a prep sink near a refrigerator drawer or cooktop, another at the children's snack center, and still another in the entertainment area. Remarkably, major manufacturers now offer sink centers that include a burner with integrated cooking vessel and set-in cutting board. Task centers combine meal planning, storage, prep, and clean-up in one flowing unit. Stylistically, the choices are seemingly endless. Materials as diverse as porcelain, enamel-coated cast iron, metal, stone, and synthetics are commonly used. Whether one-of-a-kind, free form, high style, or nostalgic, sinks are highly visible components of the total kitchen design. Likewise, faucets must perform—the stove-side pot-filler faucet is a good example—but not without a keen sense of style. Faucet handles might be polished, rubbed, or distressed, or fitted out with embellishments of stone, porcelain, or wood. It is a happy marriage of utility and artistry.

Standing Room

FLOORING

Another early step in the design process, the choice of flooring, is reliant on several factors: visual effect, functionality, and comfort. Choices range from the traditional—natural stone, ceramic or terra cotta tile, terrazzo, and wood or wood laminates—to the eclectic—cork, bamboo, or even poured concrete. Additionally, such diverse flooring elements no longer keep their distance; now they are mixed in new ways, sometimes daring, sometimes fanciful, but always interesting. Natural stone takes on a dress-up appeal with borders of small ceramic tiles or metal accents. Wood inlay might be used to delineate the outlines of large square tiles. Wood flooring can be applied straight or on the diagonal for visual effect. Planks might be broad or narrow in width, random or uniform in length, and smoothly finished or hand distressed. For comfort, in-floor heating systems keep any floor surface inviting and broaden the choices for the designer and client. Flooring selection can influence many design elements.

Surfaces are Fundamental

COUNTERS

The rules have changed, and for the better. Countertops are no longer limited to one color and one texture. Instead, they have acquired new depth and dimension in which varied materials mix and complement each other. Granite can be polished to a high gloss or honed to a satiny patina. Soapstone and limestone impart a subdued and elemental touch. Exotic woods share space with traditional butcher block. Even metals such as stainless steel and copper, and unexpected materials such as concrete, are found in the newest kitchens. Not to be outdone, synthetic surfaces, including laminates and aggregate stone-like products, give incredible flexibility in color choice. But countertops are far more interesting in a design sense: thicknesses vary; edges are rounded, ogeed, beveled, or straight; varied counter heights accommodate specific chores and, at the same time, add visual interest. An accent counter, in wood or copper, for example, creates appeal and delineates between functions. The countertop is not just the repository, but rather, a useful aesthetic of the design plan.

Illumination is Key

LIGHTING

A well-defined fixture attracts the eye, complements the overall design scheme, creates atmosphere, and sustains the personality of the room. Equally important, it sheds light on the task at hand. The ideal lighting system must do both. Chandeliers, wall sconces, and banks of pendants pull a look together. Recessed can, cove, and ambient lighting cast their own special light, but differently. Concealed under-cabinet lighting provides well-lit task spaces and highlights detailed tilework and backsplashes. To show off collectibles and illuminate glass shelving, in-cabinet lighting is perfect. Practically speaking, the choice of lighting is an elemental step in the overall kitchen design.

The Final Touch

HARDWARE

Finally, the custom kitchen is embellished with the "jewelry" of the design process: the knobs, pulls, hinges, and handles that unify and punctuate the room's individual style. Hardware might be fanciful or austere, hand wrought or cast, but it always carries with it a sense of both ornamentation and utility. Stone, metal, wood, glass, and ceramic are just some of the materials that find their way onto cabinetry. In a practical sense, the hardware chosen for the custom kitchen must be appropriate to the task at hand. Integrated appliances, for example, necessitate the use of larger handles; a dishwasher or refrigerator drawer requires hardware that is easy to grip. Likewise, for a smaller single-use cabinet, a delicate handle or pull will do. And like all jewelry, a few good pieces always make a sophisticated statement.

DESIGN

Design with
TASTE

Step Inside
THE GATHERING ROOM

There's something about a great kitchen.

Kitchens will continue to function as the multi-purpose spaces of the 21st century. And now, more than ever, they reflect the needs and sensibilities of those who use them.

They are the comfort rooms, the showplaces, the gathering spots for families and friends who come together to celebrate with food. Whether simple or elaborate, these rooms and the people who gather in them will forever make memories, both culinary and otherwise.

ARCHED TO PERFECTION

Winner National Kitchen & Bath Association's
2005 Pinnacle of Design Award
and 1st Place for Large Kitchen Category

Featured in
Women's Day Kitchens & Baths, Spring 2005

When the kitchen footprint is derived from the middle of a vast open space, the design opportunities are both liberating and cautionary, but this kitchen, an award-winning head turner, has entered the realm of the sublime. It is regal in bearing, and rich in tone and texture; however, the room also embodies a practical sensibility that reflects the unique lifestyle of the client: it functions beautifully, both as a cereal station for an on-the-go family and as a professionally fitted-out workspace for large catered affairs.

At first glance, height is the dominant feature. Two nine-foot cabinets in deep cherry flank the range; one contains a Sub-Zero refrigerator and the other, a generous pantry. Stately cherry cabinets—both massive and multipurpose—form the perimeter on the room's left. One offers glass-fronted china storage in front, two stacked microwaves and warming drawer on one side, and a built-in desk opposite. The other cabinet is fitted out for coffee and cereal breaks, with a refrigerator for milk and condiments, and a freezer drawer for ice cream and frozen treats. Close-by, a cozy banquette serves as a casual family meeting place.

The vast center island and, to its right, an equally large peninsula, offer balance plus utility: both have their own sinks and dishwashers.

The grandeur of the cabinetry is not to be outdone, however, by the carefully rendered bronze details. The ample curve of the bronze range hood is repeated in the raised platform on the island, both pieces left in their natural state to develop a patina as they age.

Cabinet and drawer hardware are bronze ovals, complementary in shape and tone to the larger bronze pieces. Their curves are realized again in the cherry v-groove ceiling and transom window. Below, cherry flooring, this time delicately distressed, anchors the space and unites the warm tones of wood and metal for an extraordinary impression.

Featured in
Midwest Living, March/April 2005 and
Northern Home & Cottages, November/December 2005

At first glance, it's linear, the unadorned expression of timeless styling, but this is a room that also resonates with rich texture and color. It's a room with a mood, one distinctly warm and elaborate. And it masters the Mission concept clearly: utility meets elegance; organization meets élan. First, the woods—cabinets and trim in quarter-sawn oak—yield a rich and intricate grain pattern. Rare American chestnut beams accentuate the ceiling. Next, the stone— abundant and diverse. Reclaimed terra cotta floor tiles in their natural state add a complementary shade and a delicate surprise: some tiles are embedded with imprints of leaves, fossils, and tiny animal tracks. Green-blue Kirkstone counters have a simple rubbed finish, their surfaces left to develop character with every use. Glazed white ceramic bricks, a retro material reminiscent of creameries and subways, form the backsplash. Mixed metals—stainless and brass— complete this remarkable setting.

Clearly, this room successfully embraces the key elements of simple style, but there is so much more at play in this design. This is a hard working kitchen that can easily accommodate a crowd—of cooks, that is. With a client who believes in group participation, helpers are not only welcome, but are also regularly pressed into service for a variety of tasks. This means that the layout must be multiple-user friendly, and it is.

A generous pantry with floor-to-ceiling shelves holds supplies. Judicial placement of drawers guarantees easy access to kitchen tools, ingredients, and potholders. Numerous sinks—three in the main counter and one in the island—are accessible for both meal preparation and clean-as-you-go chores. Countertops, the kitchen element that every serious chef covets, are generously scaled: the snack bar alone can easily accommodate ten. Friends and family, be they observers or cook's helpers, can all fit comfortably into this finely executed space.

The linear meets the vertical in this modernist space where the simple beauty of a clean line is celebrated. But, not surprising to those who appreciate the contemporary, this kitchen is decidedly warm and inviting. Generous windows, imposing in size, but elemental in design, allow natural light to flood the interior space, thus showcasing a rich mixture of woods, stone, and metals. Cabinetry is faced with Afromorsia, a stunning African veneer in a horizontal grain. The islands and perimeter cabinets are fitted with planed end pieces, a design element that is repeated throughout the house. Elongated bronze hardware provides vertical and horizontal counterpoint. French limestone floor tiles in Lagos Azul bear a custom antique finish and match the single slab fronting the fireplace.

Two islands, one a work center, the other a seating space, dominate the center of the room. The first has a single deep sink, striking in handcrafted bronze, which is under-mounted so as not to interfere with the visual line of the limestone countertop. Dishwasher drawers flank the sink and dishes are stored in two shallow base cabinets so that the dishwashers can be unloaded with one movement. The second island, primarily for seating, has a solid walnut countertop.

It's trough-shaped sink is fit for real work such as washing vegetables, and it also functions beautifully as an ice bucket or wine cooler for entertaining. Refrigerator drawers keep produce within easy reach. Against the adjacent wall, dual refrigerators flank an unusual bake center, custom-fitted for ingredients, mixing bowls, and other necessities. This modernist interpretation of the old Hoosier kitchen center has doors that hinge up instead of out, making access easy for the client, an accomplished baker.

This minimalist space provides an appropriate backdrop for an eclectic use of antiques, collectibles, and art. Flashes of red—in the island seating, dining chairs, and dishes—punctuate the space but never detract from its singular beauty.

A grand space was dedicated to this kitchen design, but the floor footprint far exceeded the wall area. The task was to create a room that was firmly delineated from the openness of the surrounding living area. The client, moreover, wanted to make a bold design statement, as well as to realize a true working kitchen that functioned especially well for entertaining and family gatherings.

The kitchen design, then, had to make its own perimeters. This was accomplished by creating a large center island that is actually anchored by its own ceiling and supports. The archways and columns give the kitchen its focus as well as its personality, borrowing as it does from the loggias of Italy. It is this unique island treatment that achieves separation, while allowing it to remain very much in the center of the surrounding living spaces.

The island ceiling is composed of honey maple panels with a large maple rosette for anchoring the bronze chandelier. The counter offers three levels: bar height for seating, sink height for prep and clean-up, and a raised maple console for display and to repeat the warm tone of the maple ceiling. It is this multi-level counter that defines the piece and provides counterpoint to its massive footprint. Practically speaking, the island is also a highly functional work center. A deep double bowl and prep sink, pullout waste receptacle, and two dishwashers handle clean-up and prep chores. On the island's adjacent side, a double sink and dishwasher increase the work capacity, and a second small waste receptacle is readily available, but discreetly out of sight. Two and one-half inch honed granite counter with profiled edges make a durable and elegant surface for work and for entertaining.

Wide crown molding forms the outer boundaries of the room. Nine-foot maple cabinets in a glazed cream finish with beveled glass doors take up an L-shaped space on one side. One full wall is dedicated to pantry storage, refrigeration, and LCD flat screen TV. The other wall is given to the commercial range with flanking upper and lower cabinetry. Eclectic details complement the design as a whole and dignify each space. The copper range hood has metal tiled fascia and a surprising backsplash of crackled glass mosaic. Copper colored bronze hardware repeats the theme of softly burnished metals. Finally, limestone tiles, as counter backsplash and as flooring, connect the elements of this singular kitchen.

It's impossible to tell that this small room is a cottage remodel, so beautifully does each component blend. Planned for a busy family of six, it uses every inch of space judiciously and creatively. The curved island, comfortable for the whole family, is geared for food preparation and clean-up. A refrigerator/freezer combination close to the cooktop completes the work triangle. The coffee maker, built into the pantry-side to the left of the refrigerator, is strategically positioned to keep countertops uncluttered and to provide easy access to a quick cup of coffee-to-go.

A beverage center features a refrigerator, icemaker, and wine cooler below, and glass-fronted storage above. To its right, a pantry and small desk with message center and large TV fit nicely into a corner.

Beyond its remarkable utility, what really captures one's attention is the abundance of style and color. Multi-use cabinets of soft green and distressed pine are distinguished by open soffits, crown molding, and beadboard accents. Open shelves contain picnic supplies and oversized serving baskets. Mullioned glass-fronted cabinets display the treasures and necessities of cottage life. Honed granite

the treasures and necessities of cottage life. Honed granite countertops in cobra green anchor and complement the cabinetry. Opposite the work zone, a farmhouse table redolent of Provence accommodates a crowd with a rustic bench on one side and a cozy upholstered seat on the other. Discreet and space-saving pocket doors to the right of the table remain hidden until needed.

SEEING RED

Featured in
Grand Rapids Magazine, November/December 2004
Log Home Design Ideas, March 2002
American Homestyle & Garden, Kitchen & Bath, Winter 1999

Sometimes a found item—in this case, an ornately detailed antique door—drives the design process. This piece once saw service as an outside door, but now finds a new and unexpected function as the pantry entryway.

Behind it, canned goods, large pots, and microwave oven stand at the ready. Built at an angle to match the placement of the range at the opposite end of the workspace, the pantry lends both symmetry and function to the kitchen footprint.

The room is executed in a rich palette of textures, colors, and patinas deliberately chosen to express a comfortable eclecticism. Distressed cabinetry in a commanding, yet muted, shade of red complements the twelve-inch square, multi-select slate on the counters and backsplash; interestingly, the tile work behind the stove continues to the high ceiling, giving the wall an uninterrupted flow. The copper range hood with an elongated stack also balances the ceiling height and adds another focal point to this diverse collection of elements. Copper pendant lights repeat its shape. A farmhouse sink, completely appropriate in this setting, is re-imagined in contemporary stainless.

The cabinetry to the right of the pantry door has the look of a country hutch but serves a dual modern purpose: a wine rack above and small refrigerator below make it a convenient area for entertaining; its compact countertop doubles as a phone and message center.

The small work island, one end supported by a slender tree trunk, includes storage, shelving, and warming drawer. It stands next to another focal point: an artisan's folk art table which increases the work space and offers yet another delightfully eclectic touch. Natural hickory flooring completes the look of this warm log home kitchen.

TONE ON TONE

Featured in
American Home Style & Garden, Kitchen & Bath, Winter 1999

The harmonious balance of this cozy room bespeaks artistic order and proportion, and its pleasing lines of French country style are further enhanced by an understated palette of similar colors. Glazed taupe cabinets, wood coffered ceiling, and wood floors are subtle gradations of the same tones. Violetta granite countertops and limestone backsplash blend smoothly. An ornate range hood with acorn and grape motif is set into the wall cavity, and to its left, a recessed area adds convenient spice storage. The island mixes seating, storage, and display ingeniously with prep and clean-up applications: its dishwasher faces tall dish storage cabinets. Convenient to the adjacent keeping room, the TV is tucked behind pocket doors in the seating island. And because this is a kitchen that entertains, a bar sink and generous open wine rack vertically flanking the refrigerator anchor an opposite wall.

MIXED METALS ARE A STANDOUT

Featured in
American Homestyle Kitchen & Bath, Spring 2000

A kitchen remodel can be fraught with difficulties and challenges, but all is forgotten when the results are as seamless as this one. Natural maple transitional cabinets are punctuated with cherry inserts. This square detailing is repeated on a larger scale in the twelve-inch square ceramic floor tiles. Highly polished granite counters are a visual counterpoint to the more subtle sheen of brushed stainless appliances. Shine of another kind is the focus of the commanding backsplash, a distressed copper and tiled frieze, its theme repeated in the smaller tiles below the upper cabinets. Their crimped edges evoke the craft of the old-fashioned tinsmith; however, there is nothing nostalgic about the display area at the end of the island: thick glass shelves and recessed lights bordered by stainless columns are fitting for an upscale art gallery.

UP AT THE CABIN

Featured in
Better Homes & Garden, Kitchen Style & Storage, Spring 2006
Midwest Living, March/April 2004
Traverse Magazine, November/December 2001

Anchored by the original pine floors and ceilings of this 1920's lakefront log cabin, this kitchen remodel remains true to its history. While it retains the homespun look, it is decidedly modern in its function and capabilities. For such a confined area, major and small appliances are tucked away as built-ins: a wine cooler is beneath the countertop; the dishwasher hides behind a golden beadboard cabinet door; and a microwave resides in a base cabinet on the island. Color, style, and texture mix happily throughout. Reclaimed red barnwood encases the range hood, while the small wall-mounted cabinet to the left of the sink emphasizes the whimsical rustic cabin theme—its narrow door is accented with chicken wire. Ample dish storage is in the adjacent hutch, a reclaimed furniture piece. Stone and tile are not to be outdone: a farmhouse sink is fashioned from a solid block of granite, its face left rough for textural counterpoint. Hand-made leaf tiles, looking for all the world as if they were swept inside by a north wind off the lake, form the backsplash and island top.

Styles and colors mix beautifully in this elegant space. Custom pieces exude the aura of antiques, yet are carefully designed for function as well as for visual impact. The cooktop is centered in a bank of cream glazed cabinets, their crown molding, pilasters, and gently turned legs reminiscent of vintage furniture. Deep drawers beneath the stove hold pots and pans, and the beautifully arched top conceals the range hood and lighting. A freestanding hutch, richly finished in deep red, stores dishes and serving pieces. The two-level cherry island, curved for seating ease and as a complement to the bowed top of the hutch, is a perfect backdrop for beautifully-carved corbels. On the prep and clean-up side, a granite counter with double sink, dishwasher, and recycle area complete the work triangle. Wide maple flooring, finished in its natural tone, ties the look together.

THE WEEKENDER

Featured in
Better Homes & Garden, Kitchen & Bath, May/June 2003

When a space is designed for relaxing, as this cottage kitchen surely is, the elements of design must evoke a sense of ease and comfort without sacrificing style or function. The palette of brights—clean white, vibrant yellow, and deep blue—catches the eye, and also sets the stage for more serious business. A galley floor plan for the work zone, bordered on one side by a butcher block island, places the range, sink, refrigerator, and small appliances all within easy reach of the cook. But this island is much more than a boundary. Its three-inch-thick maple block top is meant to be used: the marks and scratches that accumulate on the working surface will add to its character as the seasons pass at the cottage. And, while it handles prep chores and clean up with ease, the island also offers a generous bookshelf and wine rack at opposite ends, plus a comfortable place for guests to linger.

Anchoring the adjacent wall and in serious competition with the blue lake beyond, is the lightly distressed built-in hutch, a custom piece which looks like a country antique and earns its keep with abundant storage space. It easily holds the contents of a pantry, keeping small appliances and food items handy for the cook, and dishes and serving

pieces close to the dining area. The cabinets have the inset doors of vintage kitchen carpentry, but are topped with elegant crown molding, a nice complement to the ornate corbels of the range hood. Birdcage handles and pulls fashioned in wrought iron are both user-friendly and eye-catching. Ceiling and floor choices were key elements in making this room a warm and inviting retreat. Boxed beams strategically lowered the ten-foot ceiling in order to warm the space. Likewise, a mahogany-stained oak floor evokes the planks of a well-loved and well-used cottage kitchen.

Warmth fairly emanates from this kitchen and makes it an ideal spot for lingering. Honey-distressed alder wood cabinets have raised detailing for interest and varying depths to accommodate small appliances, large serving pieces, and charger plates. The intricately tiled backsplash is executed in terra cotta and cordovan colors. The island—large enough for work, family dining, and entertaining—has a cooktop, generous lower storage, and a raised mahogany L-shaped table, its gracefully turned legs evoking the craft of furniture makers. Generously scaled natural flagstone covers the floors, and above, recessed can lights in the planked wood ceiling and under-cabinet lights maintain the mood. The kitchen's desk and message center, tucked around the corner but still very much a part of the kitchen footprint, affords the client a beautiful water view.

Combining tones and styles is key to the modern kitchen, as demonstrated in this comfortable and easy mix of elements. Knotty pine, once preferred as rec room paneling, now functions beautifully underfoot. Cabinets in a soft ivory glaze are enhanced with honed marble countertops. Limestone backsplash tiles complement, but do not interfere with, a delicately mosaiced range hood. The island displays a grape motif in the carved end panels, the matching corbels, and the stools; its doors hide storage and the flush toe kick adds an important furniture detail to this fine piece. Against one wall, a bank of cabinets in distressed maple with maple countertop has the demeanor of fine furniture but works hard as varied storage. Another bank of cabinetry, this time in glazed cream, is between the kitchen and the dining room. Its arched top and glass doors are reminiscent of handcrafted cabinetry from the great homes of the past centuries, but this one is cleverly fitted with dry bar, refrigerator drawers for beverage storage and serving, as well as wide shallow drawers for table linens. To complete this look, simple bronze hardware adds understated warmth.

Even a small kitchen footprint can yield big results. This compact kitchen benefits from clean lines and tone on tone colors. An unbroken expanse of autumn brown granite for the countertops and the backsplash evoke a sense of space. Cabinets and drawers are unadorned except for beaded and mitered edges, their warm cherry finish having ample amounts of style and sophistication. Simple nickel hardware completes the look. To maintain the same clean lines and sense of space, the range hood is concealed behind cabinet panels. A two-level bar is comfortable for seating and conversation without interfering with prep and clean-up on the counter side. And for a touch of simple elegance, Art-Deco-inspired glass doors showcase fine crystal.

Can a kitchen be described as grand? Apparently so, when a work environment is as refined as this one. Centered between spacious living and family rooms, and open to both across bar-height counters, this kitchen has stunning symmetry and distinct style. A beadboard paneled ceiling and coved lights illuminate and accentuate the generous proportions of the room. Visually unique glass-sided cabinets are mounted on the countertops to maximize storage. The countertops themselves are varied in height to add interest as well as comfort for the clients, both of whom are tall. At the kitchen's center, an irregularly shaped island accommodates a massive butcher block table. Cherry floorboards yield to glazed cream cabinets, and black Uba Tuba granite counters form a vivid border around the room. Out of sight is a useful butler's pantry. A wood-burning fireplace—enclosed in glass for outdoor views—helps to define this gracious kitchen's high style.

This room plays two roles superbly: as a hard working child-friendly kitchen and as a loyal homage to pure Craftsman style. The wonderfully reminiscent design, however, does not compromise its remarkable degree of functionality. Cherry cabinetry and range hood are accented with handmade tiles, their rich green a perfect mix with the understated color palette. And while the look is authentic, the floor plan is positively inspired: matching cabinets—one a pantry, the other a perfectly disguised refrigerator and freezer— flank the cooking space. An under-counter refrigerator drawer holds beverages and snacks for the youngsters and retractable doors hide small appliances. The furniture-inspired island demands a double take, and not only for its pudding stone granite top: it has the look of a freestanding piece, but accommodates a sink—and its discreetly positioned plumbing—as well as a child level microwave oven. In a nod to the postmodern, the farmhouse sink, making a statement in bold black, lets one know that this nostalgic room is no period piece.

Sometimes a room demands close study, so nuanced are its details. Here, elegance is a given, but small, seemingly incongruous touches define it even further. The applied molding on the drawers and cabinet fronts are softened by a wealth of curves: scrolled corbels, curved fascia, and surprising, but perfectly appropriate, bun feet under the cabinets flanking the range. A commanding island displays a beautifully curved and beveled countertop. Equally unexpected, considering the vast array of hardware choices, are the simple wooden knobs on cabinets and drawers. The storage in this kitchen is abundant in both number and in size. Besides the walk-in pantry and wall-mounted cabinetry, narrow glass-doored shelves flank display areas, while underneath, diminutive drawers holds both large and small kitchen notions. Finally, warm oak flooring enriches and balances the deep greenish black of polished Uba Tuba granite counters.

Even a compact kitchen footprint can have high style, panache, and a surprising amount of room. In fact, this condominium remodel is far larger than it first appears. Stained cherry cabinetry with simple doors attracts the eye. A sense of height is attained through the uniform application of crown molding. Slender elongated hardware furthers the impression. Black granite countertops and a backsplash of white glazed subway tiles delineate the space. Proportionately-scaled appliances and range hood in brushed stainless blend with the hardware and offer a pleasing counterpoint to the deep shade of cherry. A raised bar with cherry wood top creates extra storage and shelving for displays and books, and links the open kitchen to the living area beyond.

By continuing the cabinetry into the adjacent dining space and into the step-down living area, the kitchen is visually expanded and smoothly linked to the rest of the space. Encased in cherry cabinetry, an entertainment center, wine cooler, and small refrigerator serve guests' needs and keep the kitchen free for meal preparation and clean-up chores.

OLD WORLD INFLUENCE

Featured in
Women's Day Kitchens & Baths, April 2003

When entertaining is a priority, the kitchen must meet a twofold requirement: efficiency and style, for this is a room that will host gatherings for many years to come. This kitchen meets both needs effortlessly with Old World elegance. Cherry cabinets and flooring in a burnt umber finish are reminiscent of another time. Limestone in its natural state comprises the hood surround, the sides of which meet the lower cabinets to simulate wood and stone posts. The surround's curved top is repeated in the elliptical island countertop, and again in the bowed doors of its storage space. But elegant fluted columns at its opposite end offset the curves of this piece. A glass-fronted display cabinet makes use of corbels in an unexpected way, while a generous length of smooth granite countertop and a hand-painted limestone mural behind the stove not only link the elements of wood and stone, but soften them as well.

The client, a successful restaurateur, wanted a setting that met her professional standards and made a congenial gathering place for guests. The result is a seamless melding of design and function, of style and utility. A collection of diverse materials—glass, stainless, maple, concrete, copper, and hand-glazed iridescent tiles—comes together in this incredible space of lines and curves.

Perhaps the most elemental piece and the one that inspires and informs its design, is the glass wall with glass-backed cabinets linking the kitchen to the home's greenhouse. But if the atrium draws attention to the outside, the stunning island demands attention from within. In a brilliant repetition of the parabolic theme, the two-level curved island—surfaced in concrete, of all things—is both command center and staging area. An undermounted triple sink, curved butcher block, refrigerator drawers, and rollout waste bin anchor the work side, while the upper level provides ample seating for guests. Above, the island's double level is repeated beautifully with curved wood paneling and eighteen-inch recessed ceiling detail. Curves on a smaller scale—the pullout pantry door and artisan-crafted range hood—echo the singular theme.

Surprisingly, the aura of this room, with its enormous footprint, soaring ceilings, and white-on-white palette, is at once both warm and inviting. Its secret? A clever blend of subtle design techniques that pull the space together and soften its lines and angles. Cabinets in varying heights and depths, with panel doors for storage and glass-front doors for display, are linked by crown molding. Ample curves, in the recessed alcove behind the stove, and in the island countertop, soften the kitchen's lines and angles. Arched trusses tame the imposing vaulted ceiling. While color is minimal, the cabinetry adds rich ornamentation.

The entire outer wall is given to banks of clean white upper and lower cabinets and white marble countertop. A backsplash of glazed subway tiles repeats the monochromatic theme, but with a lustrous finish. But this broad expanse of cabinetry is simply a backdrop for the grand dimensions of the ornate range hood, its supporting corbels and detailed fascia fit for a classic country house. In this generous space, the range hood's sheer size is a complement to the overall design. Wide flanking windows overlooking the lake allow bright washes of

sunlight to flood the room and give an ideal spot for bird watching.

A slab of ogeed marble, perfect for cocktails, casual dining, and buffet suppers, tops the island. Its opposite end features a massive butcher block, oiled to impart a soft sheen, and curved to match the motif repeated in the kitchen's overall theme. Another surprise—the bow-front cabinet below the butcher block—is supported by turned legs, giving it the look of an Old English sideboard. Dual island sinks—a beautiful stainless oval in the butcher block, and a stainless farmhouse design adjacent to the range top—handle prep, cooking, and clean-up. The room is anchored by satin-finished Brazilian walnut flooring.

The 5'x8' island that anchors this room and lends itself to kitchen prep, entertaining, and schoolwork, is reminiscent of the traditional farmhouse table but with a striking difference—an imposing slab of Uba Tuba granite on top and a beadboard storage center below. Local artisans fashioned the benches from reclaimed pine stumps. In a reversal of the island's color palette, the cabinets around the room's perimeter are in a deep forest green, distressed for visual interest, and then dressed up with crown molding. Granite countertops and sink, this time in a golden hue, complement the natural pine. The tall glass-fronted cabinet, a showplace for collectibles, has a beadboard interior to match the island and the backsplash beneath the upper cabinets. Behind the range, limestone tiles form a small brick pattern. Not to be overlooked for a busy family is the must-have telephone and message center that is neatly tucked into a shallow space to the left of the cooking area. Authentic flagstone flooring completes the country look.

This kitchen remodel remains true to the spirit of the historic classic Georgian home in which it is found. Its generous scale and luxurious style pay homage to those fine homes of another era, and the addition of modern conveniences brings it firmly into the realm of the 21st century.

While visual flair is important, the kitchen's many roles were given equal attention. A busy family with four children needed room for family dinners and after school gatherings, yet a serious entertainment schedule, including catered affairs, also necessitated a no-nonsense functionality in which appliances take center stage. Dual refrigerators—one stainless, the other disguised as cabinetry—serve multiple needs. Refrigerator drawers, strategically placed in the island near dual sinks, hold fresh produce. A sixty-inch range, warming drawer, steam oven, and microwave meet any cooking and prep need with ease. Dual dishwashers can be pressed into service for larger gatherings.

Besides its multiple functions, the kitchen exudes an assured sophistication. A mix of elements and colors work beautifully and

congenially within the room: jewel tones, fine wood, metals, and stone blend together to great effect. Alder wood cabinets are finished in deep red, distressed for character, and then fitted with generously elongated tumbled bronze hardware. Honed granite countertops in muted neutral—the color is called Lady Dream—offer ample workspaces. Colorful floral tiles salvaged from the previous kitchen form a bright flower basket motif behind the stove, and individual flowered tiles repeat the theme under the cabinets. Two full walls of glass fronted display cabinets act as storage and butler's pantry. Papered and lighted from within, the shelves are a perfect venue for display. Lower cabinets conceal deep-sided rollouts for storage and cloth-lined drawers for silverware.

The true focal point and the piece that commands attention for both beauty and function, however, is the island. Distressed in red on one side to match the cabinetry, it is topped with an enormous crescent bar in rich brown mahogany. Modern artisans designed the piece to resemble an antique that might have been rescued from a 19th century saloon. Its mahogany face is a fitting backdrop for elaborately carved lion corbels. Oversized stools accommodate the children, but the bar is equally at home as a serving center for gatherings. Underfoot, a floor of randomly placed limestone tiles, a preferred material in fine old homes, is both practical and elegant.

TASTE

Design with
TASTE

Elements
OF COOKING

In the kitchen.

Food plays a significant role in our lives; for sustenance, surely, but also as the centerpiece of our existence. The rituals of preparing and sharing food make us the social beings that we are. Favorite dishes enliven celebrations, honor important events, and mark holidays. A good meal has the power to evoke memories, or to even become a memory in itself.

And equally important perhaps, is the elegant symmetry of pairing these recipes with kitchen designs, for while a beautiful kitchen might be considered a piece of art by all who experience it, the kitchen is still, at its core, the American workroom. It is only given life and meaning by the people who use and enjoy it.

Inspirations.

IN 1999, I DESIGNED A COOKBOOK AS A GIFT FOR MY MOTHER
USING MANY OF OUR FAMILY RECIPES.

That experience became one of my early inspirations. When my kitchen design business began to grow, I set a long-term goal: to create another book, this time incorporating recipes with my kitchen designs. To facilitate the process, I sent past clients a kit containing a questionnaire, recipe cards, an apron, and a disposable camera. I asked them to record their thoughts about their kitchens and how they use them, including their favorite recipes. I also encouraged them to take photos of family, friends, even pets—all the important players in their lives. The result was an astonishing outpouring of enthusiasm and good will. Their participation made this book come alive.

FIRST IMPRESSIONS

Appetizers. Starters. Hors d'oeuvres. By any name, they are the prelude to a meal,

or a meal in themselves. Hot or cold, elaborate or simple, appetizers garner attention.

FRENCH QUARTER BARBECUED SHRIMP

SKEWERED SESAME BEEF

FRIED HALLOUMI CHEESE

PESTO CREAM CHEESE ROLL

BLUE CHEESE MUSHROOMS

CHEESE OLIVE BALLS

BLACK BEAN DIP

WARM FETA APPETIZER

SHRIMP MARTINIS WITH NAPA CABBAGE SLAW

WILD MUSHROOM & GOAT CHEESE BRUSCHETTA

A taste of New Orleans.

CREOLE SEASONING
Makes 14 oz of seasoning

8 oz	salt
2 oz	garlic, granulated
2 oz	black pepper, ground
1 tsp	cayenne pepper
1 tsp	thyme
1 tsp	oregano
2 oz	paprika
1 tbs	onion, granulated

SHRIMP

14	large shrimp, peeled with heads off
6 tbs	cold unsalted butter, cut into 1 oz pieces
1 1/2 tsp	black pepper, ground
1 1/2 tsp	black pepper, cracked
1 tbs	creole seasoning (above)
3 tbs	Worcestershire sauce
1 tsp	garlic, chopped
	juice of one lemon
	lemon for garnish
	French bread

1. Preheat oven to 450°

2. Mix together all Creole seasoning ingredients.

3. Place 14 large fresh shrimp, 3 tbs cold unsalted butter, ground pepper and cracked pepper, 1 tbs Creole seasoning, Worcestershire sauce, and chopped garlic in an oven-proof sauté pan large enough to scatter the shrimp in a single layer.

4. Place the pan in oven for 2 minutes.

5. Remove from the oven and sauté over moderate heat.

6. Add juice of one lemon and another 3 tbs of cold unsalted butter, stirring and swirling with a fork until done.

7. Serve the shrimp in a bowl and pour the sauce over shrimp.

8. Garnish with wedge of lemon.

9. Serve with fresh French bread.

Note: Seal leftover seasoning in an airtight container for future use.

FONDEST KITCHEN
MEMORY...
*Having guests say
"It's stunning."*

—Sue Geshel

Recipe provided by Julie Linehan
Adapted from Mr. B's Kitchen

A most delicate version of kabobs.

MARINADE

1/4 cup	soy sauce
2 tbs	sesame oil
1 tbs	Dijon mustard
1 tbs	sugar
2 tsp	garlic, minced

BEEF

8 oz	beef tenderloin, cut into 1" cubes
12	mushrooms, halved
1	large red pepper, seeded and cut into 1" pieces
2 tbs	sesame seeds, toasted

1. Stir marinade ingredients together.

2. Add cubed beef to marinade, and set at room temperature for one hour or refrigerate up to 4 hours.

3. Thread each wooden cocktail skewer with one piece of bell pepper, one beef cube, and one mushroom half.

4. Dip one side of each skewer in the toasted sesame seeds.

5. Arrange on lightly greased baking sheet and bake 5 minutes at 450°, or arrange directly on moderately hot coals for 2 to 3 minutes.

Recipe provided by Rebecca Kling

THOUGHTS ABOUT
WORKING WITH A
KITCHEN DESIGNER...
It's definitely a collaboration of your wants, dreams, wishes, and the designer's expertise. Liz's keen sense of her customer's needs and wants together with her years of experience let your vision and dreams come alive in a beautiful and functional kitchen.

—Margy Kidd

FRIED HALLOUMI CHEESE

No other cheese grills like this
Cypriot delicacy.

1	Halloumi cheese
2 tbs	flour, seasoned
2 tbs	olive oil

DRESSING

1	lime, juice and zest
1 tbs	white wine vinegar
1 tbs	capers, drained
1	clove of garlic, minced
1 tsp	grain mustard
1 tbs	fresh coriander leaves, chopped
2 tbs	extra virgin olive oil
	salt
	black pepper, coarsely cracked
	coriander sprigs for garnish

1. Unwrap cheese and pat dry with paper towel.

2. Using a sharp knife, slice it into eight slices, including the ends.

3. Prepare dressing by whisking all the ingredients together in a small mixing bowl.

4. Just before serving the Halloumi, heat the oil in a frying pan over medium heat.

5. When the oil is hot, coat each slice of cheese with seasoned flour, then add to the hot pan. Cook 1 minute on each side until golden in color.

6. Pour dressing over cheese and serve immediately on warmed plates.

Note: Good served with lightly toasted pita bread or Greek bread with toasted sesame seeds.

THOUGHTS ABOUT
WORKING WITH A
KITCHEN DESIGNER …
*I could never
have designed such a
great and beautiful
workspace. There are
so many details I
would never have
thought about;
a kitchen designer
like Liz is essential
and gives you
peace of mind.*

—Donna Roberts

Recipe provided by Leslie Banks

Smoothly satisfying in
both texture and taste.

PESTO

2 cups	packed fresh basil leaves
1 cup	pine nuts
4	garlic cloves
1 cup	olive oil
1 cup	Parmesan cheese, grated (Reggiano preferred)
1/4 cup	Romano cheese, grated
	salt and pepper

CREAM CHEESE ROLL

1-8 oz	package Philadelphia cream cheese, room temperature
1-4 oz	package chevre goat cheese, room temperature
1/2 cup	sun dried tomatoes packed in olive oil, chopped

PESTO

1. Chop basil, pine nuts, and garlic in food processor until blended.

2. While food processor is running, slowly add 1 cup of olive oil.

3. Add cheeses and process again.

4. Salt and pepper to taste.

CREAM CHEESE ROLL

1. Combine both cheeses while softened; divide into 2 balls and wrap each in wax paper.

2. Chill.

3. Roll cream cheese mixture to 1/4" thickness.

4. Spread 1/4 to 1/2 cup of pesto mixture on rolled out cream cheese.

5. Sprinkle chopped sun dried tomatoes onto pesto mixture.

6. Form cream cheese into log rolls.

7. Serve with stone wheat or rice crackers.

Note: Pesto can be used for other dishes.

Recipe provided by Mary Ann Lassiter
Adapted from Dallas Morning News recipe

FONDEST KITCHEN
MEMORY...
My husband loves to
cook in this kitchen,
too; that was worth it.

—Sue Hartemayer

BLUE CHEESE MUSHROOMS

Mushrooms are a simple, yet elegant repository for this delicious cheese.

2 lbs	white mushrooms
2 to 3 jars	Kraft roka blue cheese

1. Clean mushrooms with a mushroom brush or paper towel. (Do not wash in water).

2. Remove stems.

3. Fill the cavity of each mushroom with Kraft roka blue cheese.

4. Place on a cookie sheet and put under broiler until cheese is browned and bubbly (approximately 4 to 5 minutes).

5. Serve warm.

FAVORITE KITCHEN
FEATURES …
*The granite countertop
peninsula is a
beautiful example of
perfectly integrated
form and function.*

—JULIE LINEHAN

Recipe provided by Barb Johnson
From a neighbor's recipe

A blend of flavors and textures
for the palate.

1/4 lb	cheddar cheese
1/4 cup	butter
3/4 cup	flour
1/8 tsp	salt
1/2 tsp	paprika
	pimento-stuffed green, kalamata, black, or Greek olives, pitted

1. Preheat oven to 400°.
2. Mix first five ingredients together.
3. Using the hand, roll small amount of dough around the olives to form a small ball.
4. Continue until all dough is used.
5. Bake on an ungreased cookie sheet for 15 minutes.

Recipe provided by Pat Summers

ADDITIONAL
THOUGHTS…
Isn't this the
best kitchen ever?

—John & Nancy Banks

BLACK BEAN DIP

Rich, creamy, and hearty.

I can	black beans, drained and mashed	
1/2 cup	sour cream	
1/4 cup	lime juice	
4	garlic cloves, minced	
I tsp	chili powder	
	cheddar cheese, shredded	
	tortilla chips	

1. Mix all ingredients.
2. Top with shredded cheddar.
3. Serve with tortilla chips.

Note: "My kids' favorite dip!"

Recipe provided by Julee Zook

Oh, those Greeks
and their wonderful cheese.

1/2 lb	block of feta cheese
1	clove of garlic, minced
1	plum tomato, seeded and finely diced
1/2	red pepper, finely diced
1/2	green pepper, finely diced
1 tbs	red onion, finely diced
1/2 tsp	dried oregano
1 tbs	fresh flat leaf parsley, chopped
	salt and pepper to taste
1 to 2 tbs	olive oil
	pita triangles or hearty wheat crackers

1. Place the block of feta cheese in a 9" microwave-safe pie plate.

2. Top feta with garlic, tomato, red and green pepper, and red onion.

3. Sprinkle with oregano, parsley, salt, and pepper.

4. Drizzle olive oil over the top.

5. Microwave 1 to 11/2 minutes or until feta is slightly soft.

6. Remove from microwave and serve with pita triangles or hearty wheat crackers.

Note: This recipe may be assembled 2 or 3 days in advance and stored in the refrigerator.

Recipe provided by Jan Marshall
Adapted from Ellis Island Catering

KITCHEN DESIGN
DREAMS AND GOALS...
The kitchen is the first thing one sees upon entering the house. It shows who lives here. Our kitchen has always held the "business of daily life."

—Julee Zook

Stirred, not shaken.

It's safe to indulge in these beautiful seafood cocktails.

SHRIMP

24	unpeeled large fresh shrimp (about 1 1/2 lbs)
2	large eggs, lightly beaten
1/2 cup	soft breadcrumbs
1 1/4 cup	sweetened flaked coconut, toasted
4 cups	vegetable oil

SLAW

1/2 cup	mayonnaise
2 tbs	lite soy sauce
1 tbs	dark sesame oil
4 cups	Napa cabbage, shredded
1	large carrot, shredded
1	red bell pepper, cut into very thin strips
2 tbs	sesame seeds, toasted
	lime for garnish

SHRIMP

1. Peel shrimp, leaving tails on; de-vein, if desired.
2. Dip shrimp in egg.
3. Stir together breadcrumbs and coconut; dredge shrimp in mixture.
4. Pour oil into a dutch oven; heat to 375°.
5. Fry shrimp in batches over medium high heat 2 minutes or until golden.
6. Drain on paper towels.

SLAW

1. Whisk the first three slaw ingredients in large bowl.
2. Add cabbage, carrot, and pepper, tossing to coat.
3. Sprinkle with sesame seeds.
4. Spoon Napa cabbage slaw evenly into 8 martini glasses.
5. Top each with 3 fried shrimp.
6. Garnish with lime wedges, if desired.

THOUGHTS ABOUT
WORKING WITH A
KITCHEN DESIGNER...
*A kitchen is an
important room in the
house, and it's the
most used room in our
house. I didn't have
time or money to
waste in making
mistakes.*

—Kristi Penman

Recipe provided by Kim & Jill Kueffner
Adapted from Southern Living Magazine recipe

WILD MUSHROOM & GOAT CHEESE BRUSCHETTA

"Bruscare" means to toast over coals.
Wild mushrooms and chevre make a subtle addition.

16	French sour baguette slices
4 oz	goat cheese
2 tbs	olive oil
1 tbs	unsalted butter
2	large garlic cloves, minced
2	shallots, peeled and minced
2 oz	oyster mushrooms
4 oz	shiitake mushrooms
5 oz	portabella mushrooms
1/4 cup	sherry
1/4 cup	chicken stock
1 tsp	fresh thyme
1/2 tsp	fresh basil
	kosher salt and red pepper flakes to taste
	lemon zest, minced
	chives, minced

1. Preheat broiler. Brush the baguette slices with the softened room temperature goat cheese and set aside.

2. Sauté garlic and shallots in the olive oil and butter until softened.

3. Add coarsely chopped mushrooms to the pan and sauté for a minute or two.

4. Add the rest of the ingredients and sauté until most of the moisture evaporates.

5. Layer mushroom mixture on the goat cheese baguettes and broil for 2 to 3 minutes until warmed through.

6. Garnish with lemon zest and chives.

Robin Morris
Whitecaps Restaurant

FONDEST KITCHEN MEMORIES…
Christmas time. Cooking for 10-12 kids after skiing. Shopping and cooking together for the kids and their friends.

—Christina Vidosh

Salads & Sides

ACCOMPANIMENTS

Each of these sides can act as the companion piece to the main course,
or as a memorable dish in its own right.

FIESTA SALAD

ROASTED CORN & BLACK BEAN SALAD

GRILLED PORTABELLA & SPINACH SALAD

HOMEMADE CAESAR SALAD

MIXED GREEN SALAD

BEST-IN-THE-WEST BAKED BEANS

CHINESE CHICKEN SALAD

SPINACH GRATIN

ORZO PARSLEY GRATIN

PRONOZ

PARTY POTATOES

HASSELBACK POTATOES

FIESTA SALAD

As wonderful to look at
as it is to eat.

VINAIGRETTE

1/2 cup	shallots, chopped
1/4 cup	fresh lime juice
1/4 cup	fresh cilantro, chopped
1 tbs	garlic, minced
1/2 cup	canola oil

SALAD

3 cups	red leaf lettuce
3 cups	romaine lettuce
2	plum tomatoes, chopped
1/2	red bell pepper, thinly sliced
1/2	yellow bell pepper, thinly sliced
1/2	avocado, diced
1/4 cup	red onion, thinly sliced
1/4 cup	corn kernels, cooked
1/3 cup	tortilla chips
1/2 cup	white cheddar, shredded
1/4 cup	pumpkin seeds

VINAIGRETTE

1. Prepare and combine vinaigrette ingredients.
2. Shake or whisk together.

SALAD

1. Wash lettuces and tear into salad-size pieces.
2. Add tomatoes, peppers, avocado, onions, and corn.
3. Mix all above ingredients.
4. Crumble tortilla chips (or leave whole for presentation).
5. Toss with vinaigrette or leave dressing on side for individual application.
6. Sprinkle with cheese and pumpkin seeds.

KITCHEN DESIGN
DREAMS AND GOALS...
Keep it simple,
efficient, casual, and
low maintenance!

—Susie Simon

Recipe provided by Kristi Penman

ROASTED CORN & BLACK BEAN SALAD

From the Southwest direct to your table.

2 cups	fresh corn kernels (3 ears of corn)
15 oz	can of black beans, rinsed and drained
1 cup	tomato, chopped
1/2 cup	lime juice
1/4 cup	red onion, finely chopped
1/2	jalapeno pepper, seeded and chopped
2 tsp	hot sauce
1/2 tsp	salt
1/2 tsp	ground cumin
1/2 tsp	ground coriander
1/2 tsp	pepper

1. Place corn on foil-lined baking sheet.
2. Broil corn 5" from heat 12 minutes or until lightly browned, turning over once.
3. Remove from oven, and let stand 10 minutes.
4. Slice corn from cobs.
5. Combine corn and remaining ingredients in a large bowl.
6. Cover and chill until ready to serve.

Note: Best made a few hours ahead so flavors can blend.

Recipe provided by Jane Von Voigtlander

FAVORITE KITCHEN ELEMENTS…
No matter where I put the food, people end up in the kitchen around our wonderful island.

—Barb Johnson

GRILLED PORTABELLA & SPINACH SALAD

The meaty Agaricus bisporus mixes beautifully with these greens.

LEMON PEPPER VINAIGRETTE

1/2 cup	lemon juice, freshly squeezed
2 tbs	red wine vinegar
1 cup	olive oil
1 tsp	fresh garlic, minced
1 tsp	salt
1 1/2 tsp	black pepper, coarsely cracked

SALAD

8	portabella mushroom caps
	olive oil for grilling
2	handfuls of spinach, trimmed and rinsed
2 oz	Parmesan cheese, shaved
12	cherry tomatoes, cut in half

VINAIGRETTE

1. Place all ingredients in a small bowl.
2. Whisk together.

SALAD

1. Prepare grill or preheat broiler.
2. Brush mushrooms with olive oil.
3. Grill or broil mushrooms until tender, 3 to 4 minutes.
4. Toss spinach with vinaigrette.
5. Stack a small pile of spinach on salad plates.
6. Layer shaved Parmesan, then a mushroom; repeat layers, pressing down to keep from falling.
7. Drizzle with vinaigrette.
8. Garnish with cherry tomato halves.
9. Serve while mushrooms are still warm.

FAVORITE KITCHEN
FEATURES…
*Our kitchen is very
well-planned. The
color is so pleasing,
and everything is
convenient. It turned
out better than I
imagined.*

—Mary Pizzimenti

*Recipe provided by Carrie West
Adapted from
At Blanchard's Table cookbook recipe*

The preparation of this bold dressing has always been an event in itself, and rightly so.

DRESSING

4	anchovy fillets
3	cloves of garlic, peeled
2 tbs	olive oil
1 tsp	Worcestershire sauce
1 tsp	Dijon mustard
1/2 tsp	hot pepper sauce
1 1/3 cup	real mayonnaise
1/2 cup	Parmesan cheese, freshly grated
2 tbs	fresh lemon juice
	salt and pepper

SALAD

3	hearts of romaine
2 cups	croutons

1. Combine anchovy fillets, garlic, oil, Worcestershire sauce, mustard, and hot pepper sauce in blender.
2. Blend until mixed thoroughly.
3. Whisk in mayonnaise, 2 tbs of cheese, 2 tbs lemon juice, salt and pepper.
4. Put lettuce in a large bowl.
5. Toss with dressing, remaining cheese and croutons.

Recipe provided by Christina Vidosh

THOUGHTS ABOUT
WORKING WITH A
KITCHEN DESIGNER…
I definitely think a designer is necessary. The knowledge and talent are unlimited. The way Liz worked magic in our kitchen was priceless.

—Mary Birdsell

MIXED GREEN SALAD

Simple elegance.

1 bunch	mixed greens
1/2 cup	dried cranberries
1/3 cup	crumbled blue cheese
	balsamic vinegar
1-2	pears, sliced
1/2 cup	sugar pecans
3 tbs	sugar

Recipe provided by Glenda Jehle

SALAD

1. Mix all ingredients.
2. Toss with balsamic vinegar.
3. Top with sliced pear and pecans.
4. Serve.

SUGARED PECANS

1. In a small saucepan, cook 1/2 cup of pecans with 3 tbs of sugar over low heat.
2. Stir constantly until pecans are coated and sugar is dissolved; watch carefully.
3. Cool.

BEST-IN-THE-WEST BAKED BEANS

The potluck staple puts on its party hat.
An old favorite, all dressed up.

1 lb	bacon, cut in pieces
1	large onion, chopped
1/2 cup	ketchup
1/2 cup	favorite barbecue sauce
4 tbs	prepared mustard
4 tbs	molasses
1 tsp	pepper
2 16 oz	cans each of light kidney beans, pork and beans, and butter beans

1. Brown bacon and onion.
2. In a crock-pot or baking dish, combine ketchup, barbecue sauce, mustard, molasses, and pepper.
3. Add browned bacon, onion, and beans.
4. Bake 1 hour at 350° or in a slow cooker for the day.

FONDEST KITCHEN
MEMORY...
*My first cup
of coffee on
December 12, 2003,
when, after 19 months,
we were back in
our own house.*

—Pat Summers

Recipe provided by Debbie Nactrab

A taste of the orient.

DRESSING

4 tbs	sugar
4 tbs	vinegar
2 tsp	salt
1/2 tsp	pepper
1/2 cup	salad oil
1 tbs	sesame oil

SALAD

4	chicken breasts
4	green onions, thinly sliced
1	head lettuce, thinly sliced
1/2	package wonton wrappers
	cooking oil
1/4 cup	sesame seeds
1	small bag sliced almonds

DRESSING

1. Combine sugar, vinegar, salt, and pepper; mix or shake until dissolved.
2. Add salad and sesame oils to vinegar mixture; then mix or shake.

SALAD

1. Preheat oven to 350°.
2. Bake chicken in oven 60 minutes or until done; then shred.
3. Slice green onions and lettuce.
4. Fry wonton wrappers in oil until lightly browned.
5. Place sesame seeds and almonds under broiler 2 to 3 minutes.
6. Combine all prepared salad ingredients in brown bag, add salad dressing, and shake.
7. Serve immediately.

Recipe provided by Amanda Bosco

FONDEST KITCHEN
MEMORY…
Once our project was complete, we had our first gathering. Everyone brought their famous food dishes. They instinctively went to our island/buffet area to set up, then migrated to our entertaining/bar area. Not once did someone question where things should be! Then, as the last person arrived I heard, "Man, the food actually looks better in this kitchen."

—Julee Zook

SPINACH GRATIN

Tangy spinach makes a fine pairing with freshly grated Parmesan and Gruyere cheese.

4 tbs	unsalted butter
4 cups	yellow onions, chopped (2 large)
1/4 cup	all purpose flour
1/4 tsp	nutmeg, grated
1 cup	heavy cream
2 cups	milk
5 10 oz	packages chopped, frozen spinach, thawed
1 cup	Parmesan cheese, freshly grated
1 tbs	kosher salt
1/2 tsp	black pepper, freshly grated
1/2 cup	grated Gruyere cheese

1. Preheat oven to 425°.

2. Melt butter in a heavy bottomed sauté pan over medium heat.

3. Add onions and sauté until translucent, about 15 minutes.

4. Add flour and nutmeg and cook, stirring for 2 more minutes.

5. Add cream and milk and cook until thickened.

6. Squeeze as much liquid as possible from the spinach and add the spinach to the sauce.

7. Add 1/2 cup of the Parmesan cheese and mix well.

8. Season to taste with the salt and pepper.

9. Transfer spinach to a baking dish and sprinkle the remaining 1/2 cup Parmesan and the Gruyere on top.

10. Bake for 20 minutes, or until hot and bubbly.

11. Serve immediately.

Note: This dish is creamy on the inside and browned and crunchy on the top. You can assemble the dish with the cheese topping a day or two ahead; then cover, refrigerate, and bake at specified temperature an additional 5 minutes.

THOUGHTS ABOUT
WORKING WITH A
KITCHEN DESIGNER...
*While I had ideas of
what I wanted, the
kitchen designer may
offer a better solution
for my dream.*

—Lynda Panaretos

Recipe provided by Helen Stroud
Adapted from Barefoot Contessa Parties recipe

A new twist on pasta.

1 lb	orzo (rice shaped pasta)
6	garlic cloves
1 cup	heavy cream
1 cup	canned chicken broth
1 cup	Parmesan, freshly grated
1 1/2 cup	fresh parsley, minced
4 tbs	dry bread crumbs
3 tbs	cold unsalted butter

1. Preheat oven to 325°.
2. In a kettle of boiling salted water, boil orzo with the garlic (do not peel), until "al dente."
3. Drain in a colander.
4. Rinse orzo well under cold water and drain well again.
5. Remove garlic cloves, peel, and mash with a fork.
6. In a large bowl, whisk mashed garlic with cream.
7. Add orzo, broth, 3/4 cup Parmesan, garlic cream, 1 cup parsley, salt and pepper to taste, and combine mixture well.
8. Transfer mixture to a buttered 2-quart baking dish and smooth the top.
9. In a small bowl, toss the breadcrumbs with the remaining 1/4 cup Parmesan and 1/2 cup parsley.
10. Sprinkle mixture evenly over orzo mixture and dot the top with the butter, cut into very thin slices.
11. Bake for 1 hour and 15 minutes, or until it is bubbly around the edges and the top is golden.

Recipe provided by Jan Marshall

FONDEST KITCHEN
MEMORY...
*It has to do with my
husband, and we
weren't cooking!*

—sujo Offield

PRONOZ

*Spinach and cheese combine beautifully
in this family favorite.*

6	eggs
6 tbs	flour
24 oz	cottage cheese
8 oz	package Old English sharp cheese, cut into 1" squares
1 or 2	packages chopped, frozen spinach, thawed

1. Preheat oven to 350°.
2. Slightly beat eggs.
3. Thaw spinach and squeeze out water.
4. Mix eggs and spinach with flour and cheeses.
5. Put into 21/2 quart dish.
6. Bake for 1 hour.

Note: Perfect for holidays with ham or turkey dinners. I cut leftovers into bite size pieces and serve as an hors d' oeuvre.

Recipe provided by Sue Geshel
Mom's recipe

PARTY POTATOES

*Everyone has a version of this popular side.
Feel free to embellish.*

2 lb	frozen hash browns
1	can of cream of chicken soup
1 pt	sour cream
10 oz	cheddar cheese, grated
1/2 cup	onion, chopped
1/2 cup	melted butter

1. Preheat oven to 350°.
2. Sauté onion in butter.
3. Add onion to all other ingredients.
4. Put mixture in casserole dish.
5. Bake uncovered for 40 minutes.

Note: Feeds a crowd. Kids love this dish.

FAVORITE KITCHEN
FEATURES...
*"Big Red" is a
favorite of all who
come here. The blend
of wood, stone, metal,
and color is simply the
best kitchen ever. A
few have even tried to
duplicate, but all we
can say is "nice try."*

—John & Nancy Banks

Recipe provided by Pam Ziegel
Mom's recipe

HASSELBACK POTATOES

When in Stockholm, try the original recipe at
Hasselbacken restaurant.

6	large uniform baking potatoes
3 tbs	butter, melted
	lemon pepper to taste
	salt to taste
1/4 cup	Parmesan and/or Asiago cheese, freshly grated
2 tbs	dry bread crumbs
	parsley for garnish

1. Preheat oven to 375°.

2. Scrub or peel potatoes.

3. Slice a portion off of the bottom of the potato to stabilize during baking and plating.

4. Make 1/8" thick slices 3/4 of the way through the potato.

5. Place potatoes in a greased baking dish.

6. Brush surface of the potatoes with butter.

7. Sprinkle with salt and pepper.

8. Bake for 45 minutes.

9. Remove from oven and sprinkle with finely-grated cheese and bread crumbs.

10. Bake 15 to 20 minutes longer until potato is done and crust is slightly browned.

11. Garnish with parsley and serve immediately.

Recipe provided by Denise White

FONDEST KITCHEN
MEMORY
Family nights with
everyone in the
kitchen at Christmas
time. The big center
island full of cookie
dough and decorations
and the grandchildren
sitting all around
decorating their own
Christmas cookies.

—Donna Roberts

Soups

SIMPLE, SOPHISTICATED, OR SUBLIME

Soup is the original comfort food, so it's no wonder that every culture has a wealth of soup recipes.
As a starter or a main dish, soup is always satisfying.

BUTTERNUT SQUASH SOUP & SEARED SCALLOPS

SPLIT PEA WITH HAM

LOBSTER CORN CHOWDER

WHITE CHICKEN CHILI

WILD RICE SOUP

BEER CHEESE SOUP

APRÈS STEW

EASY MINESTRONE SOUP

ALL-AMERICAN CHILI

SPINACH BISQUE

GREEK MELANGE

GRAMPY'S STEW

BUTTERNUT SQUASH SOUP & SEARED SCALLOPS

*Sweetness from the garden
and the ocean.*

2 tbs	unsalted butter
2 tbs	good olive oil
4 cups	sweet yellow onions, chopped (3 large)
2 tbs	Madras curry powder
5 lbs	butternut squash (2 large)
1 1/2 lbs	crisp baking apples (4)
2 cups	water
2 tsp	kosher salt
1/2 tsp	fresh ground pepper
2 cups	apple cider
1/2 lb	per person – large sea scallops

1. Warm butter and olive oil in a large covered stockpot.

2. Add onions and curry powder; cook uncovered for 15 to 30 minutes, or until onions are tender.

3. Stir occasionally.

4. Peel squash, cut in half and remove the seeds.

5. Cut squash into chunks.

6. Peel, quarter, and core apples; cut into chunks.

7. Add squash, apples, salt, pepper, and 2 cups of water to the pot.
Use 1 cup of water and 1 cup of chicken stock, if desired.

8. Bring to a boil, then cover, reduce the heat to low, and cook 30 to 40 minutes, until squash and apples are soft.

9. Process soup through a food processor fitted with stem blade.

10. Poor the soup back into the pot.

11. Add apple cider and enough water to make soup the desired consistency. (Should be slightly sweet, thick, and spicy.)

12. Add salt and pepper to taste.

13. Sear sea scallops on med-high heat, browning both sides until cooked through.

14. Place 3 to 4 scallops per bowl on top of soup and serve hot.

Note: Add cumin or fresh ginger to vary flavor.

FAVORITE KITCHEN
FEATURES…
*If it's cooking with
the kids, wrapping
presents, doing
paperwork, or
entertaining friends,
there always seems to
be enough room to get
the job done…The
island is our favorite
design element
—the center
of the action.*

—Julee Zook

Recipe provided by Dana Selis

A rich and hearty traditional.

1 lb	split peas
3 tbs	unsalted butter
1 cup	yellow onion, chopped
1/2 cup	celery, chopped
1/2 cup	potato, chopped
1/2 cup	carrot, chopped
2 tsp	garlic, minced
1	ham hock
1/2 lb	smoked ham, chopped
1 tsp	salt
3/4 tsp	fresh ground pepper
1/4 tsp	red pepper flakes, crushed
8 cups	chicken broth
1	bay leaf
2 tsp	fresh thyme

1. Cover peas in water for 8 hours or overnight. Drain.

2. In a large pot, melt butter over medium high heat.

3. Add onions; cook for 2 minutes.

4. Add celery, potato, and carrots; cook about 3 more minutes.

5. Add garlic and cook for 30 seconds.

6. Add ham hock and ham; cook for 2 to 3 more minutes.

7. Add drained peas, salt, pepper, and pepper flakes; stir for 2 minutes.

8. Add 8 cups of chicken broth, bay leaf, and thyme.

9. Cook until peas are soft and potato is disintegrating; about 1 hour.

10. Remove bay leaf before serving.

Note: Add more broth or water if too thick.

People who say they don't like pea soup will change their minds.

Recipe provided by John and Nancy Banks

THOUGHTS ABOUT
WORKING WITH A
KITCHEN DESIGNER…
*…it pulls everything
together and makes it
all work efficiently.*

—Barb Johnson

LOBSTER CORN CHOWDER

A Maine boiled dinner
minus the shell and the cob.

4-5 1 lb	lobster tails
6	ears of corn on the cob (3 1/2 cups kernels)
1/2 lb	slab smoked bacon, with rind
8	sprigs of fresh thyme
1 tsp	whole black peppercorns
4	bay leaves
1	onion, peeled for stock
3	medium onions, cut in large 3/4" dice (3 cups)
4 tbs	unsalted butter
8	small new potatoes (1 lb), red or white, cut in 1/3" slices
1 1/2 cup	heavy cream
	salt and freshly ground black pepper
	chives or parsley, chopped for garnish

1. Bring a generous amount of salt water to a boil, enough to cover lobsters completely when they are added.

2. When water is at a rolling boil, add lobsters.

3. Bring back to boil and cook lobsters 3 minutes exactly. Drain.

4. Cool lobsters and remove all meat.

5. Cut tails in half lengthwise and remove the intestinal tracts.

6. Cut meat into large bite-size pieces; set aside in the refrigerator.

7. Put all shells in a large kettle and cover with 12 cups water; bring to a simmer.

8. Cut corn off cobs; set aside.

9. Cut cobs across and add to kettle. (Do not add the kernels.)

10. Remove bacon rind and add to kettle; set bacon aside.

11. Pick leaves off fresh thyme and set aside; put stems of thyme in kettle.

12. Add peppercorns, bay leaves, and whole onion to kettle.

13. Simmer for 1 hour and 15 minutes.

14. Strain the stock – approximately 6 to 7 cups.

15. Dice bacon into 1/4" pieces and render in kettle until crisp.

16. Add diced onions, thyme leaves, and butter; cook until onions are wilted and tender (about 6 minutes); do not brown.

17. Add corn, potatoes, and stock; simmer about 20 minutes or until potatoes are cooked through.

18. Add cream and lobster meat. Season to taste with salt and pepper, and simmer 2 minutes more.

19. Serve in soup plates with chunks of ingredients sticking out above broth. Sprinkle each bowl with chopped chives or parsley.

Note: Roasting corn in bacon renderings adds extra flavor.

Add 4 dashes of Tabasco sauce for a little kick.

KITCHEN DESIGN
DREAMS AND GOALS...
To have my
'big girl' kitchen.

—sujo Offield

Recipe provided by Denise White

The new favorite.

1 1/2 lbs	boneless skinless chicken breast
2 tbs	garlic, chopped
2 cups	onions, chopped
1 tbs	oil
4 cups	chicken broth
1	can chilies, chopped
2 tsp	cumin, heaping
2 tsp	oregano
1/4 tsp	cayenne pepper
2 dashes	Tabasco sauce
1 48 oz	jar of great northern beans

1. Bake chicken breast in 350° oven for 30 minutes.
2. Let cool, then cut into bite size pieces.
3. In a soup pot, soften garlic and onions in oil.
4. Add chicken broth, chilies, cumin, oregano, cayenne pepper, and Tabasco sauce.
5. Stir in beans and chicken.
6. Bring to a boil, and then simmer for 15 minutes. Stir frequently.
7. Serve with cornbread and/or corn chips and shredded Monterey Jack cheese.

Note: Homemade chicken broth is best.

Recipe provided by Barb Johnson

KITCHEN DESIGN
DREAMS AND GOALS…
We wanted to incorporate the natural materials and high quality decor from the living/dining room area as part of the kitchen, making it one large area.

—Cathy Scriven

WILD RICE SOUP

There is nothing as substantial as the nutty sweetness of this favored rice.

6 tbs	butter
I tbs	onion, minced
1/2 cup	flour
3 cups	chicken broth
2 cups	cooked wild rice
1/2 tsp	salt
1/3 cup	ham, minced
1/3 cup	carrots, finely chopped
I cup	half and half
2 tbs	dry sherry (optional)
3 tbs	slivered almonds, chopped

1.   Melt butter in saucepan.

2.   Sauté onion until tender.

3.   Blend in flour.

4.   Gradually stir in broth.

5.   Cook, stirring constantly until mixture comes to a boil.

6.   Boil and stir I minute.

7.   Stir in rice, salt, ham, and carrots.

8.   Simmer about 5 minutes.

9.   Blend in half and half and sherry.

10.   Heat to serving temperature.

11.   Add almonds.

Notes: More ham can be used.

Add more chicken broth if soup is too thick.

Recipe provided by Susie Simon
From friend, Patricia Harstad

Hops add a marvelous flavor
to this hearty blend.

2 cups	potatoes, diced
1 1/2 cup	onion, chopped
1 cup	carrots, thinly sliced
1 cup	celery, chopped
2 cups	water
1/4 cup	butter
6	chicken bouillon cubes
2 cups	milk
1/2 cup	flour or Wondra flour
3 cups	cheddar cheese, grated
1 tsp	dry mustard
1/2 cup	beer

1. Combine first seven ingredients and bring to boil.

2. Boil until vegetables are tender.

3. Mix together milk and flour and gradually add to soup.

4. Gradually add the last three ingredients.

5. Let cheese melt and remove from heat.

6. Serve.

FONDEST KITCHEN
MEMORY...
The caterer said it was
his favorite kitchen to
work in. Now there's a
testimonial.

—Linda Johnson

Recipe provided by Mary Birdsell

APRÈS STEW

For the end of a fine day.

4	white onions, sliced
3 lb	shoulder of lamb, cut into 1 1/2" cubes
8	carrots, peeled and sliced
8	celery ribs, sliced
6	potatoes cut into 1/3" slices
2 cups	chicken, veal, or beef stock
2 cups	white or red wine (dry)
1 1/2 tsp	fresh rosemary (or 1/2 tsp dried rosemary)
	salt and pepper to taste
	parsley, chopped for garnish

1. In a large pot, place a layer of sliced onions, then lamb cubes, carrots, celery, and potatoes.
2. Season layers with salt, pepper, and dry rosemary. (If using fresh rosemary, add during last 30 minutes of cooking.)
3. Repeat the layers.
4. Finish with potatoes as the top layer.
5. Pour in enough stock and wine to cover the layers.
6. Bring stew to a boil; skim off any fat that comes to the top.
7. Lower heat and cover pot.
8. Let stew simmer for 2 1/2 to 3 hours, or until lamb is tender.
9. Stir occasionally and add more stock or wine if needed.
10. Serve in large soup bowls and garnish with chopped parsley.

Note: Serve with a salad and crusty bread.

FONDEST KITCHEN
MEMORY...
*Friends. Friends.
Friends. Cooking
together and sharing
special occasions.*

—Barb Johnson

Recipe provided by Nadine Hellings

A simple version of the Italian classic.

1 32 oz	can chicken stock
2 cans	Veg-all
1	package chopped, frozen spinach
1 can	stewed tomatoes
1 can	diced tomatoes
1 can	cannellini beans
1 cup	macaroni noodles
1/2 cup	Parmesan cheese, grated

1. Combine chicken stock, Veg-all, spinach, tomatoes, and cannellini beans in soup pot.
2. Cook on low for 45 minutes.
3. Thicken by using wand blender or place in electric blender.
4. Add macaroni and cheese.
5. Cook on low for additional 30 minutes.
6. Serve in large bowls with crusty Italian bread.

Recipe provided by Gail Young

FONDEST KITCHEN
MEMORIES…
*Family gatherings—
everyone helping to
create a great,
enjoyable meal.*

—Nadine Hellings

ALL-AMERICAN CHILI

The nation's contribution to comfort food.

6 oz	hot turkey Italian sausage
1 lb	ground sirloin
2 cups	onion, chopped
1 cup	green bell pepper, chopped
8	cloves of garlic, minced
1	jalapeno pepper, chopped
2 tbs	chili powder
2 tbs	brown sugar
1 tbs	ground cumin
3 tbs	tomato paste
1 tsp	dried oregano
1/2 tsp	freshly ground black pepper
1/4 tsp	salt
2	bay leaves
1 1/4 cup	merlot or other fruity red wine or beef broth
2 28 oz	cans chopped/diced tomatoes
2 15 oz	cans kidney beans, drained, or chili beans not drained
1/2 cup	shredded cheese

1. Remove casings from sausage.

2. Combine sirloin, sausage, onion, green pepper, garlic, and jalapeno pepper in dutch oven over medium-high heat.

3. Cook 8 minutes or until sausage and beef are browned, stirring to crumble. (Also very good with just 1 1/2 lbs ground sirloin and no sausage.)

4. Add next 8 ingredients.

5. Cook for 1 minute, stirring constantly.

6. Stir in wine or broth, tomatoes, and beans, and bring to a boil.

7. Cover, reduce heat, and simmer 1 hour, stirring occasionally.

8. Uncover and cook for 30 minutes, stirring occasionally.

9. Discard bay leaves.

10. Sprinkle each serving with cheddar cheese.

FAVORITE KITCHEN
ELEMENTS...
We love everything about our kitchen and pantry. The creative layout that Liz designed was one we had not considered and couldn't be happier with. We love to work together and this well-thought-out space allows us to do so.

—Kathleen &
Larry Acker

Recipe provided by Kristi Penman
Adapted from Cooking Light

Rich, creamy,
and a visual delight.

2 10 oz	packages chopped, frozen spinach
4 cups	chicken broth
3 tbs	onion, chopped
1/2 cup	butter
4 tbs	cornstarch
1 cup	cheddar cheese, grated
2 cups	half and half
4 tbs	Parmesan cheese, grated

1. Cook spinach in chicken broth until tender, about 10-15 minutes.

2. In separate pan, sauté onions in butter until soft.

3. Let cool and add cornstarch, stirring until blended.

4. Add sautéed onions to spinach and broth.

5. Stir in grated cheese, half and half, and Parmesan cheese.

6. Simmer, stirring until the flavors are blended.

Recipe provided by Pam Johnson
Adapted from Bountiful Arbor,
Ann Arbor Junior League cookbook recipe

KITCHEN DESIGN
DREAMS AND GOALS...
Function was my first
goal. I wanted a
kitchen that worked
for my daily needs and
also one that would
serve as the 'hub'
during both casual
and formal gatherings.
It was also very
important to me that
my kitchen would have
a feeling of warmth—
that it would be a
place that was so
inviting that everyone
would want
to be there.

—Sandy Kasischke

GREEK MELANGE

*Only the Greeks could invent this
wonderful medley of flavors.*

6 tbs	olive oil
1/4 cup	onions, finely chopped
1 clove	garlic, finely chopped
1 28 oz	can whole tomatoes, drained and chopped
1/2 cup	white wine
3 tbs	fresh parsley, chopped and divided
1/2 tsp	oregano
	salt and pepper to taste
1 1/2 lbs	medium fresh shrimp, shelled and de-veined
5 oz	feta cheese, cut into 1/4" cubes

1. In a heavy skillet, sauté onions in oil for 5 minutes.

2. Stir in garlic, tomatoes, wine, 1 tbs parsley, oregano, salt, and pepper.

3. Bring to a boil; cook uncovered until thickened, about 15 to 20 minutes.

4. Add shrimp; cook over moderate heat 5 minutes or until pink.

5. Stir in cheese and sprinkle on remaining parsley.

*Recipe provided by Pam Johnson
Adapted from Bountiful Arbor,
Ann Arbor Junior League cookbook*

THOUGHTS ABOUT
WORKING WITH A
KITCHEN DESIGNER...
*They can pull the
space together, so that
every inch is used
wisely.*

—Nadine Hellings

A dish from the heart.

2 lbs	beef tenderloin
	cooking oil
1	medium white onion, diced
	garlic, chopped
2 tsp	flour
	salt and pepper to taste
1 jar	spaghetti sauce
	water
1 can	tomato soup
1 can	stewed tomatoes (optional)
4	carrots, sliced
4	large potatoes, peeled and chopped
1/3 cup	10-minute barley
1 can	corn
1 can	green beans
1 can	peas

1. In a large stew pot, add cooking oil; brown onion and garlic.
2. Cut 2 lbs of beef tenderloin into 1/2" cubes.
3. Toss meat with flour, salt, and pepper.
4. Add seasoned meat to pan and brown on medium high heat.
5. Add one jar of favorite spaghetti sauce with the same amount of water.
6. Add one can of tomato soup, with a can of water, and one can of stewed tomatoes.
7. Bring to a boil.
8. Cover with lid vented, and reduce heat to simmer.
9. Cook slowly for 1 1/2 to 2 hours.
10. In a separate stock pot, boil carrots and potatoes until barely tender.
11. Add 10-minute barley to stock pot and cook.
12. Combine stock pot ingredients to meat mixture.
13. Add cooked corn, peas, barley, and green beans to meat mixture; combine. (May use any veggies you like.)
14. Continue to simmer until stew is heated completely through.

Note: Serve with or over buttered egg noodles, with a side green salad and homemade bread. A perfect Sunday dinner in front of a fire.

Recipe provided by Beth Fisher
Family recipe

FONDEST KITCHEN
MEMORY...
Cooking for my entire family...a joyful time.

—Pat Summers

Breads & Brunch

A FAVORED REPAST

Not too early; not too late. Brunch is an excellent occasion for a variety of hearty fare. This favored time 'twixt breakfast and lunch is a perfect venue for fancy breads and unexpected mains. Go ahead: mix flavors and textures for crowd-pleasing variety.

CHEESE BREAD

ULTIMATE BREAD STICKS

PIZZA BREAD

VIENNA STUFFED BREAD

SWEET CORN BREAD

CREAM CHEESE BANANA NUT BREAD

OVERNIGHT FRENCH TOAST SUPREME

BREAKFAST CASSEROLE

GRANDMA'S PANCAKES

MOM'S CEREAL

SAUSAGE AND CHEESE GRITS CASSEROLE

GLAZED COFFEE CAKE

CHEESE BREAD

Rich enough by itself,
but try it with sweet creamery butter on top.

1 3/4 cup	water
1/2 cup	cornmeal
2 tsp	salt
1/2 cup	molasses
1	package yeast
1/2 cup	water
2 tbs	butter
4-5 cups	flour
1 lb	Kraft American cheese, cubed

1. Preheat oven to 350°.

2. Dissolve yeast in 1/2 cup lukewarm water; set aside.

3. Combine water, corn meal, and salt in 2-qt. sauce pan.

4. Bring to a boil; stir continuously until slightly thickened.

5. Remove from heat.

6. Stir in molasses and butter.

7. Cool to lukewarm.

8. Add molasses/cornmeal mixture to yeast mixture; combine.

9. Gradually add flour to form stiff dough.

10. Knead on floured surface until smooth and satiny—about 5 minutes.

11. Let rise 1 1/2 hours, covered with towel.

12. Divide dough in two.

13. Roll dough out, sprinkle with cheese cubes and form into 2 round loaves.

14. Line two 9" round pans with foil, extending foil over sides of pan; grease well with butter and sprinkle with cornmeal.

15. Put one loaf in each pan.

16. Let rise 60 minutes, until double in size.

17. Bake for 45 to 55 minutes.

Note: Kraft American can be substituted with Boar's Head or other processed cheese.

Slice, butter, and place under broiler to toast—great for breakfast, too.

THOUGHTS ABOUT
WORKING WITH A
KITCHEN DESIGNER...
Finding a designer
who can artistically
interpret your needs
and desires is key.
We found this talent in
Liz Firebaugh.

—Kathleen &
Larry Acker

Recipe provided by Mary Birdsell

Ultimately excellent.

1	package Pillsbury breadstick dough
1/2 cup	onion, finely chopped
4 oz	tomato and basil feta cheese
8	slices of bacon cut in half, uncooked

1. Preheat oven to 375°.

2. Line cookie sheet with foil and cover with non-stick spray.

3. Unroll and separate breadsticks.

4. Cut breadsticks in half crosswise and place on baking sheet.

5. Press onion and cheese into dough.

6. Wrap with bacon.

7. Bake 15 to 20 minutes.

Note: Can be served as an appetizer.

Recipe provided by Nadine Hellings
From family friend, Kristian McAuliffe

FONDEST KITCHEN
MEMORY...
> *Sitting with friends around the island— cooking, drinking wine, talking, and enjoying being in a warm and comfortable kitchen.*

—Kristi Penman

PIZZA BREAD

*This hearty, savory loaf
goes fast in a crowd.*

2	frozen bread loaves, thawed
1 1/2 lbs	ground round
15 oz	can tomato sauce
1	can mushrooms, sliced
	garlic powder to taste
1	green pepper, thinly sliced
	pepperoni, sliced
	mozzarella cheese, shredded

1. Preheat oven to 350°.

2. Brown ground round and drain.

3. Add tomato sauce, salt, pepper, and garlic powder to meat.

4. On a cookie sheet greased with shortening, spread bread dough into oblong shape.

5. Place meat with sauce, peppers, mushrooms, cheese, and pepperoni on bread dough.

6. Fold and seal on top and ends.

7. Bake for 25 minutes.

THOUGHTS ABOUT
WORKING WITH A
KITCHEN DESIGNER…
*Every single inch has
to be planned; there
are so many details
only a professional
can know the how, the
why, and the where.
And all of the new
gadgets coming out—
who can keep ahead
of it all?*

—Susie Simon

*Recipe provided by Mary Pizzimenti
Created with a friend*

VIENNA STUFFED BREAD

*The Viennese tradition of fine eating
is redolent in this satisfying bread.*

1	French baguette
8 oz	grated cheese (any combination)
1/2 cup	butter, melted
1 tbs	dry mustard
1 tbs	poppy seed
2 tbs	onion, diced
1/2 tsp	Lawry's seasoned salt, or to taste
1/2 tsp	lemon juice

1. Preheat oven to 350°.

2. Slice loaf horizontally, almost all the way through.

3. Layer cheese inside loaf.

4. Put loaf back together again.

5. Slice bread on the diagonal almost all the way through, and place on foil.

6. Melt butter and mix with the remaining ingredients.

7. Pour butter mixture over bread.

8. Wrap loaf in foil and bake for 30 to 40 minutes. Reheat if made ahead.

Note: Bread can be frozen before baking. If frozen, bake an extra 5 minutes.

*Recipe provided by Sandy Kasischke
Adapted from Clock Wise Cruise, 1984
Junior League of Detroit recipe*

FONDEST KITCHEN MEMORY . . .
Planning a "gourmet" lunch with my granddaughters for the adults in the family.

—Cathy Scriven

SWEET CORN BREAD

Cornbread taken to the next level.

1/2 cup	salted butter
1 cup	sugar
2	eggs
1 cup	yellow cornmeal
1 1/2 cup	flour
2 tsp	baking powder
1/2 tsp	salt
1 1/2 cup	buttermilk

1. Preheat oven to 375°.

2. Cream butter and sugar until smooth.

3. Beat in eggs to mix.

4. Alternate the rest of the dry ingredients with the buttermilk to mix.

5. Bake 30 to 40 minutes, until a toothpick comes out dry.

Note: My husband claims he married me for this recipe.

FONDEST KITCHEN
MEMORY…
*We created a memory
for all time in our new
kitchen this summer
when Lauren (age 15),
Kathryn (age 12), and
I baked fresh summer
berry pies: a double
crust blueberry and a
lattice top cherry!
Yum!*

—Kathleen Acker

Robin Morris
Whitecaps Restaurant

CREAM CHEESE BANANA NUT BREAD

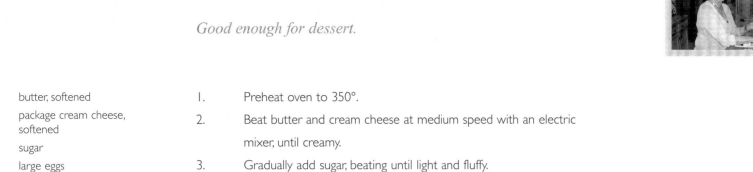

Good enough for dessert.

3/4 cup	butter, softened
8 oz	package cream cheese, softened
2 cups	sugar
2	large eggs
3 cups	all purpose flour
1/2 tsp	baking powder
1/2 tsp	baking soda
1/2 tsp	salt
1 1/2 cup	mashed bananas (about 4 medium)
1 cup	pecans, chopped and toasted
1/2 tsp	vanilla

1. Preheat oven to 350°.
2. Beat butter and cream cheese at medium speed with an electric mixer, until creamy.
3. Gradually add sugar, beating until light and fluffy.
4. Add eggs, one at a time, beating until blended.
5. Combine flour and next 3 ingredients; gradually add to butter mixture, beating at low speed just until blended.
6. Stir in bananas, pecans, and vanilla.
7. Spoon batter into two greased and floured 8"x4" loaf pans.
8. Bake for 1 hour or until a long wooden pick inserted in center comes out clean and sides pull away from pan. (Shield with aluminum foil for the last 15 minutes to prevent browning, if necessary.)
9. Cool bread in pan on wire racks 10 minutes.
10. Remove from pans.
11. Cool 30 minutes on wire racks before slicing.

Recipe provided by Connie Grazanka

KITCHEN DESIGN
DREAMS AND GOALS...
    ...we wanted a kitchen that would be the 'heart' of our home. We wanted a working kitchen as well as a space for entertaining, eating a family meal, hanging around, doing homework projects, cooking together, and having coffee with a friend.

—Tina Griffin

OVERNIGHT FRENCH TOAST SUPREME

This make-ahead dish is both easy and elegant.
A beautiful start to the day.

1	loaf fresh cinnamon bread (Alanson Bakery)
4	eggs
2	egg yolks
3/4 cup	sugar
4 cups	half and half
1 tbs	vanilla
1/2 cup	butter, melted

1. Preheat oven to 350°.
2. Cut bread into large cubes and place in buttered 9"×13" pan.
3. Pour 1/4 cup melted butter over bread.
4. Combine eggs, egg yolks, sugar, half and half, and vanilla.
5. Whisk together well and pour over bread.
6. Add another 1/4 cup melted butter over top.
7. Press bread down into pan and cover tightly with plastic wrap.
8. Refrigerate overnight.
9. Bake for 25 minutes or until custard is set.
10. Cool 10 minutes.
11. Cut into serving-sized pieces and serve with warmed maple syrup.

Note: This is a breakfast staple for guests who visit during the summer. They come back for seconds every time. My friend shared this recipe with me several years ago. It's a girdle buster – but worth every bite.

FAVORITE KITCHEN
ELEMENTS...
The blending of granite,
stainless steel, and
cherry wood cabinets.

—Carol & Jim Stroud

Recipe provided by Linda Johnson
Borrowed from friend, Laura Richards

BREAKFAST CASSEROLE

*There is no easier way
to satisfy and impress a morning crowd.*

1 lb	sausage
6-8 slices	white bread
1	small can sliced green chilies, drained
3/4-1 cup	grated cheese (Swiss or cheddar)
4 oz	can mushrooms, drained
6-8	eggs
2 cups	half and half
1 tsp	prepared mustard
	salt and pepper

1. Preheat oven to 350°.
2. Fry, drain, and crumble sausage; set aside.
3. Place 6-8 slices of white bread in greased 13"x9"x2" pan.
4. Top with green chilies, cheese, mushrooms, sausage, salt, and pepper.
5. Mix 6-8 eggs with half and half and prepared mustard.
6. Pour egg mixture over bread base.
7. Refrigerate overnight.
8. Bake for 45 to 60 minutes.
9. Serve warm.

Recipe provided by Wendy Crilly
Family recipe

THOUGHTS ABOUT
WORKING WITH A
KITCHEN DESIGNER...
*They think of things
and solve problems
that we could not.
They are a very
important part
of a successful
kitchen plan.*

—Pam Ziegel

GRANDPA'S PANCAKES

A cherished morning memory.

6	eggs
1/2 tsp	salt
1 1/2 tsp	sugar
1 1/2 cup	flour
23/4 cup	milk
1 tbs	oil

1. Beat eggs with hand beater until blended.

2. Mix in remaining ingredients just until smooth.

3. Grease heated griddle if necessary.

   (To test griddle, sprinkle with a few drops of water. If bubbles skitter around, heat is just right.)

4. Pour about 3 tbs of batter from tip of large spoon or from a pitcher onto hot griddle.

5. Cook pancakes until puffed and dry around edges.

6. Turn and cook other side until golden brown.

Note: Pancakes will be thin.

A family recipe Liz and her dad have made since she was a little girl.

FONDEST KITCHEN MEMORY...
July 4th with friends preparing their dishes, baking, and finally setting out all the food on the island. As the sun set, everyone went to the beach for the bonfire, fireworks and hummers.

—Lynda Panaretos

Recipe provided by Frances Hansen

MOM'S CEREAL

Eat your breakfast.

1	large container old fashioned Quaker Oats
4 oz	package chopped pecans
4 oz	package chopped walnuts
4 oz	package chopped almonds
1 cup	honey
1 cup	water
1/4 cup	canola oil
1/3 Jar	wheat germ

1. Preheat oven to 350°.

2. Put oats and nuts in large roasting pan.

3. Mix together water, honey, and oil, and heat in microwave for 2 minutes.

4. Pour liquid mixture over oats and nuts and stir until thoroughly mixed.

5. Sprinkle wheat germ and mix well.

6. Bake for 20 minutes, longer if you prefer it crunchy. (Be careful; it will burn easily.)

7. Let cool and transfer into an easy-pour container; store in the refrigerator.

Recipe provided by Kathleen Acker

FAVORITE KITCHEN
FEATURES…
*It can handle large
crowds comfortably,
yet it feels very cozy
for just two of us.*

—Libby Follis

SAUSAGE & CHEESE GRITS CASSEROLE

Southern comfort.

1 lb	Jimmy Dean's sausage, browned
	Tabasco sauce to taste
1/2 tsp	salt
1/8 tsp	pepper
1 cup	instant grits
2 cups	water, boiling
1 cup	extra sharp cheese, grated
1/4 cup	butter, melted
2	large eggs, beaten
8 oz	can mild green chilies, seeded and chopped
	salsa for topping

1. Preheat oven to 350°.
2. Brown sausage and drain well.
3. Add Tabasco sauce, salt, and pepper; set aside.
4. Cook grits in 2 cups boiling water.
5. Add all ingredients together, stirring until well mixed.
6. Pour mixture into a well-buttered 9"x12"x2" baking dish.
7. Bake uncovered for 1 hour.

THOUGHTS ABOUT
WORKING WITH A
KITCHEN DESIGNER...
*It was a great
experience to know
that a professional
was planning our
kitchen. Many ideas
were incorporated
that we did not
think about. It was a
great collaboration!*

—Jan Marshall

*Recipe provided by Carrie West
Mother-in-law's recipe*

GLAZED COFFEE CAKE

A sweet start to the day. Serve to family and friends,
or wrap one in a beautiful basket for a hostess gift.

DOUGH

1	package yeast
1/4 cup	lukewarm water
1/4 cup	evaporated milk
1	egg, unbeaten
1/4 cup	currants (optional)
2 1/4 cups	flour
2 tbs	sugar
1 tsp	salt
1/4 cup	cold butter

FILLING

1/4 cup	soft butter
1/2 cup	brown sugar
1/2 cup	walnuts or pecans

FROSTING

2 tbs	butter
1 cup	powdered sugar
1-2 tbs	evaporated milk
1/2 tsp	vanilla

1. Preheat oven to 350°.
2. Dissolve yeast in water in large bowl.
3. Mix milk, egg, and currants; add to yeast-water mixture.
4. Mix flour, sugar, and salt in separate bowl; cut in cold butter with pastry blender; gradually add yeast mixture.
5. By hand or with dough hook, mix until dough becomes a cohesive ball.
6. Place in buttered bowl.
7. Cover and refrigerate 2 hours or up to 2 days.
8. Divide dough into thirds. Roll each to a 12"x6" rectangle.
9. Mix butter and brown sugar together; spread on rectangle.
10. Sprinkle nuts on top.
11. Roll up each rectangle starting at the 12" side. Seal. Shape into crescents. Place on parchment covered baking sheet. Cut outer edge halfway into dough about 1" apart. Turn the cut edges with a quarter twist.
12. Let rise for 45 minutes.
13. Bake for 20 to 25 minutes.
14. Brown butter lightly. Beat till smooth with powdered sugar, evaporated milk, and vanilla. Spread on coffee cakes.

Note: Can be frozen for one or two months. Defrost. Warm gently in oven or microwave.

Recipe provided by Helen Lundstrom

FONDEST KITCHEN
MEMORY...
Early morning pajama
and pancake "parties"
with our visiting
nephews.

—Julie Linehan

Meat Poultry Fish

THE MAIN ATTRACTION

Meat, poultry, and fish are staples in the American kitchen,
but they can be tricked out in surprising ways. Seasonings, marinades,
vegetables, and pastas impart a special touch to these dishes.

PORK TENDERLOIN WITH PEACH COMPOTE

CORNISH PASTY

BALSAMIC MARINATED BEEF TENDERLOIN

LAMB SHANKS

BARBECUE BEEF BRISKET

ITALIAN CHICKEN BREASTS

DEVILED SALMON CAKES

ROLLADEN

DAVE'S DEVILED STEAK

DRIED CHERRY WHITEFISH

SHRIMP RISOTTO WITH SPINACH & BASIL

ASIAN GRILLED SALMON

MOLASSES-GRILLED RIB EYE STEAKS

PORTUGUESE SOPAS

*A perfect blend of
sweetness and textures.*

COMPOTE SAUCE

3 tbs	butter
1/2 cup	fresh sage, chopped (set 2 tbs aside for seasoning pork, reserve remainder for peach compote)
4 cups	frozen peaches, thawed and diced
4 tsp	green peppercorns in brine, drained and coarsely chopped
1 tbs	packed brown sugar

MEAT

4	pork tenderloins, cleaned and trimmed (approximately 1 1/2 lbs each)
1/4 cup	olive oil
2 tbs	fresh thyme, chopped (save remaining thyme sprigs for garnish, if desired)
	kosher salt and freshly ground pepper to taste

COMPOTE SAUCE

1. In small saucepan, melt butter over medium heat.
2. Add reserved sage, peaches, peppercorns, and brown sugar.
3. Sauté for about 5 minutes or until peaches are tender and flavors are melded.
4. Season to taste with salt and pepper.
5. Set aside for up to 1 hour, or cover and refrigerate for up to 24 hours; reheat before serving.

MEAT

1. Brush pork tenderloins with olive oil on both sides, and sprinkle with 2 tbs of sage and thyme.
2. Salt and pepper tenderloin to taste.
3. Grill tenderloins over medium-hot coals or on gas-fired grill, until desired temperature.
4. Slice on diagonal and place on platter.
5. Garnish with thyme sprigs.
6. Serve compote on the side.

FAVORITE KITCHEN
ELEMENTS...
*I love a double oven, a
great island, and a
cool backsplash*

—Christina Vidosh

Recipe provided by Peggy Brown

The original pocket sandwich pays homage to the workingman's lunch.

PASTRY

5 cups	flour
2 cups	vegetable shortening
1 tbs	salt
1 1/2 cup	water (approximately)
1/2 cup	milk (set aside for coating pasty before baking)

FILLING

2	medium potatoes, quartered and thinly sliced
1	medium onion, minced
1/4 cup	rutabaga, thinly sliced (optional)
2 lbs	round steak cut into very small cubes
	salt
	pepper
	Lawry's salt

1. Preheat oven to 425°.
2. Mix flour and salt in large bowl.
3. Mix in shortening by hand until texture resembles coarse crumbs.
4. Add water all at once and work into pastry ball.
   (Add more water if needed; mixture should be very moist.)
5. Wrap in wax paper and chill in refrigerator.
6. Spray 2 baking sheets with non-stick cooking spray.
7. Using chilled pastry, form approximately 3" ball for each pasty and roll out on floured surface to form an 8" to 10" round.
8. Place rounds (one at a time) on baking sheet and fill half the round with a generous cup of filling, leaving a 1" edge.
9. Fold unfilled half over the filling. (Bottom edge should slightly overlap top edge forming a half moon shape.)
10. Pinch to seal and remove any excess pastry.
11. With your hand, pat each pasty with milk.
12. Cut a small 1" slice in the center of each pasty and insert a pat of butter.
13. Bake 10 minutes at 425°, then reduce heat to 350° for 30 minutes.
14. Cool 15 minutes covered with a kitchen towel, and serve with ketchup, chili sauce, and sweet pickle relish.

Makes 8 pasties

Note: Dan's grandmother, Cora Mitchell Gould, taught our daughters how to make the same pasties that she made for her father and brothers to take for their lunch in the mines in Copper Mountain, Michigan. This was not only a hearty meal, but by wrapping the pasties in newspaper, they helped to keep the men's hands warm.

Recipe provided by Candy Sebold
From Dan's grandmother,
Cora Mitchell Gould

FONDEST KITCHEN
MEMORIES...
*There are many,
however I had a
"girlfriends' weekend"
and Liz joined us for
dinner in the kitchen
she designed—great
food and laughter.*

—Libby Follis

BALSAMIC MARINATED BEEF TENDERLOIN

This famous cut is enhanced by
a rich sweet and sour finish.

1 lb	center-cut beef tenderloin
1 tbs	kosher salt
1/4 cup	balsamic vinegar
1/4 cup	dry red wine
1	large shallot, coarsely chopped
1 tsp	rosemary, coarsely chopped
1 tsp	sage, coarsely chopped
1/4 tsp	pepper, freshly ground
1 tsp	vegetable oil

1. Rub salt over tenderloin for 1 to 2 minutes.

2. Refrigerate uncovered for 1 hour.

3. In blender, puree vinegar, wine, shallot, rosemary, sage, and pepper.

4. Put meat in small stainless steel baking dish.

5. Pour marinade over meat, rubbing off the salt.

6. Refrigerate for 1 hour, turning and basting every 15 minutes.

7. Coat grill with oil using damp paper towel.

8. Remove meat from marinade and grill over medium-hot fire, turning occasionally, until browned and medium rare – about 15 minutes or until meat thermometer registers desired temperature.

9. Transfer to a cutting board and let stand for 10 minutes.

10. Strain balsamic marinade into a small stainless steel saucepans; bring to a boil over moderately high heat and simmer for 30 seconds.

11. Slice the beef tenderloin and serve with sauce.

KITCHEN DESIGN
DREAMS AND GOALS...
*We wanted
contemporary beauty
with functionality.*

—Carol & Jim Stroud

Recipe provided by Kristi Penman

Delicate and tender.

4	meaty lamb shanks, trimmed
1/2	lemon
1/4 tsp	garlic powder to taste
1 cup	flour
2 tsp	salt
1/2 tsp	pepper
1/2 cup	salad oil
1	can condensed beef consomme
1 cup	water
1	medium yellow onion, chopped
4	carrots, peeled and cut in chunks
4	stalks of celery, cut in chunks

1. Preheat oven to 350°.

2. Rub lamb with lemon and sprinkle with garlic powder. Let stand 10 minutes.

3. Combine flour, salt, and pepper in a paper bag and shake shanks one at a time to coat; then save the flour.

4. Brown shanks in hot oil in large heavy skillet; remove and set aside.

5. Add 4 tbs of seasoned flour to pan drippings and stir flour until browned.

6. Add consomme and water; stir and cook until slightly thickened.

7. Add onion.

8. Place shanks in one layer in large baking dish or roasting pan, and pour consomme mixture over them. Refrigerate until ready to use.

9. Place in oven uncovered for 90 minutes.

10. Turn shanks, add carrots and celery and continue to bake an additional 60 minutes.

Recipe provided by Tina Griffin
Mother-in-law's Recipe

THOUGHTS ABOUT
WORKING WITH A
KITCHEN DESIGNER...
I had a general idea of what I wanted. Kitchen designers are able to take it a step further, making the most of space, design elements, up-to-the-minute appliances, and the added flair to make a good idea a fantastic result.

—Linda Johnson

BARBECUE BEEF BRISKET

Eastern Europe meets American Southwest.

9-11 lbs	beef brisket, fat trimmed	
2 tbs	liquid smoke	
	salt and pepper	
3 tbs	brown sugar	
1	large bottle catsup	
1/2 cup	water	
4 tbs	Worcestershire sauce	
3 tsp	dry mustard	
2 tsp	celery seed	
6 tbs	butter, melted	

1. Preheat oven to 300°.

2. Rub liquid smoke, salt, and pepper on both sides of trimmed beef brisket.

3. Wrap in foil and refrigerate overnight.

4. The next day, place brisket, wrapped in foil, into a large pan.

5. Bake for approximately 4 hours.

6. Prepare sauce by combing brown sugar, catsup, water, Worcestershire sauce, dry mustard, celery seed, and butter.

7. Heat sauce mixture to boil.

8. Slice and serve with sauce.

Note: A July 4th favorite.

FAVORITE KITCHEN
ELEMENTS…
*The huge center
island, designed to
look like it was
taken out of
an old Irish pub.
Family and friends
can "belly up"
on one side
while staying out
of the prep area.*

—Linda & David
Johnson

Recipe provided by Lynda Panaretos

ITALIAN CHICKEN BREASTS

The Italians know something about pollo.

4	boneless chicken breasts
1/2 cup	ricotta cheese
2 tbs	Parmesan cheese
1 tbs	green onion, sliced
1/4 tsp	dried basil
1/4 tsp	dried oregano
1/8 tsp	dried thyme
1/8 tsp	salt
2 cups	spaghetti sauce
1 cup	shredded mozzarella

1. Preheat oven to 350°.
2. Pound each chicken breast to 1/4" thickness.
3. In a small bowl, combine remaining ingredients except spaghetti sauce and mozzarella.
4. Mix well and spread a quarter of mixture on each chicken breast.
5. Fold in sides and roll up.
6. Secure with wooden picks.
7. Arrange in 9" square pan seam side down.
8. Pour favorite spaghetti sauce over chicken, top with mozzarella and foil.
9. Bake for 40 minutes.
10. Serve over pasta.

Recipe provided by Donna Roberts
Adapted from Cranbrook Reflections recipe

FONDEST KITCHEN
MEMORY...
*Baking cookies with
my grandsons.*

—Gail Young

DEVILED SALMON CAKES

Full of flavor and a new take on salmon.

2 7.5 oz	cans of salmon, drained
1/2 cup	onion, diced
1/2 cup	corn kernels, fresh-cooked, canned or thawed
	salt and freshly ground black pepper to taste
1/2 cup	mayonnaise
1 tbs	Dijon mustard
1 tsp	pickle relish, drained
1 tsp	fresh lemon Juice
1/2 tsp	Worcestershire sauce
1/4 tsp	paprika
2 dashes	Tabasco sauce
1	egg
1 1/2 cup	saltine cracker, crushed into crumbs
2 tbs	unsalted butter
2 tbs	corn oil
	light lemon yogurt sauce, for serving (mix a little lemon zest with yogurt)

1. Carefully flake salmon into a bowl, discarding any small bones, cartilage, and skin.

2. Add onion, corn, salt, and pepper; fold together with rubber spatula and set aside.

3. In bowl, combine mayonnaise, mustard, pickle relish, lemon juice, Worcestershire sauce, paprika, and Tabasco sauce. Fold these ingredients into salmon mixture.

4. Lightly beat egg. Using rubber spatula, fold into salmon mixture along with 1/2 cup of cracker crumbs. Place remaining cup of cracker crumbs on a dinner plate.

5. Form salmon mixture into eight 3" patties. Carefully coat them with cracker crumbs. Refrigerate, loosely covered, for 1 hour.

6. Melt butter with oil in 10" non-stick skillet over medium heat. Cook salmon cakes, four at a time, for 3 to 4 minutes per side, pressing down slightly on them with the back of a spatula and adding more butter or oil to the skillet if necessary. Drain on paper towel.

7. To serve, spoon light lemon yogurt sauce onto center of 8 medium-sized plates. Place a salmon cake atop the sauce in center of each plate. Serve immediately.

Note: When adding diced vegetables to the flaked salmon, fold ingredients together gently so that the salmon doesn't break up.

THOUGHTS ABOUT
WORKING WITH A
KITCHEN DESIGNER...
*Designers can help lay
out and prioritize the
amount of space and
storage for
your personal
requirements—
tailor made!*

—Julee Zook

Recipe provided by sujo Offield

ROLLADEN

A specialty of southern Germany.

2 lbs	round steak (cut as thin as possible)
	salt and pepper to taste
	garlic, fresh or powder
1	medium sweet onion, thinly sliced
1/2-1 lb	bacon
1	can beef gravy

1. Preheat oven to 350°.

2. Pound round steak to tenderize.

3. Salt, pepper, and garlic to taste.

4. Place layer of onion, then layer of bacon on round steak.

5. Roll tightly and tie in 2 to 3 spots.

6. Bake in covered pan for 1 hour.

7. Remove from oven and pour off fat.

8. Lower oven to 300°

9. Pour can of gravy over meat, and return to oven for 30 minutes.

Recipe provided by Rita Johnacheck

FONDEST KITCHEN MEMORY...
Cooking class I did for 12 homeschoolers. Laughter and fun all afternoon. I'm going to make it an annual event.

—Susie Simon

DAVE'S DEVILED STEAK

Beef made unforgettable.

2 lbs	sirloin steak, boneless, cut 2" thick
2 tsp	lemon juice
2 tbs	prepared mustard
	Lawry's seasoned salt to taste
1/4 cup	catsup
1/4 cup	water
1/4 cup	olive oil
2 tbs	wine vinegar
2 tbs	soy sauce
3 tbs	cherry jam
3 tbs	brown sugar
	black pepper, freshly ground to taste
	Tabasco sauce

1. Combine lemon juice with prepared mustard and spread on both sides of steak.

2. Sprinkle generously with seasoned salt.

3. Combine catsup, water, olive oil, wine vinegar, soy sauce, cherry jam, brown sugar, pepper, and a few drops of Tabasco sauce; heat until boiling.

4. Pour sauce over steak.

5. Allow to stand 2 hours or longer, turning occasionally.

6. Bring steak to room temperature before grilling.

7. Prepare coals.

8. When fire is ready, grill steaks 9 minutes each side (18 minutes total). Allow steak to rest a few minutes for a beautiful rare center.

9. Slice in 3/8" to 1/2" strips and serve.

FONDEST KITCHEN
MEMORY...
*We were fortunate to
have our whole family
here for Christmas. It
was so special! Liz
had planned the
kitchen so well that we
were not in each
other's way.*

—Mary Birdsell

*Recipe provided by
David and Linda Johnson
Adapted with an old friend
from Junior League Cookbook recipe*

A cold water species with delicate taste.

SAUCE

I cup	dried cherries
I cup	dry vermouth
1/2 tsp	garlic, minced
I tbs	shallots, chopped
I tbs	unsalted butter
1/4 cup	heavy cream
I tbs	whole grain mustard

FISH

4-6	whitefish fillets
	salt, pepper, and paprika to taste

SAUCE

1. Combine cherries and vermouth in saucepan.
2. Reduce over heat and set aside.
3. Sauté garlic and shallots in butter.
4. Add cream and mustard to sauté pan; stir and heat.
5. Add dried cherries and vermouth reduction to cream sauce.
6. Keep sauce warm until fish is baked.

FISH

1. Preheat oven to 375°.
2. Place filets in shallow baking sheet.
3. Brush with melted butter.
4. Sprinkle salt, pepper, and paprika to taste.
5. Bake for 8 to10 minutes.
6. Spoon sauce over fish and serve.

Note: This sauce should be enough for 4 to 6 servings.

Cooking time may very depending on the size and thickness of filets.

Often, we double the sauce recipe because it is so good.

Recipe provided by Margy and Wally Kidd,
and children, Katie and Tommy

FAVORITE KITCHEN
ELEMENTS...
The design provides
an abundance of
counter space and
storage. My cabinets
are beautiful. I can't
select something that I
like most because I
like everything so
much!

—Sandy Kasischke

SHRIMP RISOTTO WITH SPINACH & BASIL

Sweet creamy rice in harmony with tender shrimp,
herbs, and greens.

6 cups	low-salt chicken broth
1 lb	uncooked large shrimp, peeled and de-veined
2 tbs	olive oil
1 1/2 cup	onion, chopped
2	large garlic cloves, minced
1 1/2 cup	arborio rice or medium-grain white rice (about 9 1/2 oz)
1/2 cup	dry white wine
6 oz	package fresh baby spinach leaves
1/2 cup	freshly grated Parmesan cheese, plus additional for passing
1/4 cup	fresh basil, chopped

1. Bring 6 cups of broth to simmer in medium saucepan.
2. Add shrimp.
3. Turn off heat, cover, and let stand until shrimp are just opaque in center – about 3 minutes.
4. Using slotted spoon, transfer shrimp to small bowl; cover with foil to keep warm.
5. Cover broth to keep warm.
6. Heat oil in heavy large saucepan over medium heat.
7. Add onion and sauté until tender – about 5 minutes.
8. Add garlic and stir 1 minute.
9. Add rice and stir until edge of rice is translucent but center is still opaque – about 2 minutes.
10. Add wine and cook until absorbed, stirring occasionally – about 2 minutes.
11. Add 3/4 cup warm broth and simmer until almost all broth is absorbed, stirring often – about 2 minutes.
12. Continue to add broth, 3/4 cup at a time, until rice is just tender and mixture is creamy, stirring often and allowing almost all broth to be absorbed after each addition – about 25 minutes total.
13. During last 5 minutes, add spinach in 4 batches, stirring and allowing spinach to wilt after each addition.
14. Mix shrimp, 1/2 cup cheese, and basil; add to rice mixture.
15. Season with salt and pepper.
16. Spoon risotto into shallow bowls and serve, passing additional cheese separately.

FONDEST KITCHEN
MEMORY…
…finally moving in
after completion.

—Laura Steele

Recipe provided by Carol Stroud

ASIAN GRILLED SALMON

Another secret of the Orient.

1	side fresh salmon, boned (about 3 lbs)
2 tbs	Dijon mustard
3 tbs	soy sauce
6 tbs	olive oil
1 tsp	garlic, minced

1. Heat grill.

2. Cut salmon into 6 pieces.

3. Whisk together all of the ingredients and drizzle onto salmon.

4. Allow to sit for 10 minutes.

5. Grill for 4 to 5 minutes, then turn carefully and grill for another 4 to 5 minutes.

6. Serve warm, room temperature or chilled.

Note: Use best quality mustard, soy sauce, and olive oil for optimum flavor.

Recipe provided by Libby Follis

FONDEST KITCHEN
MEMORY...
Chuck made me homemade scones in our new kitchen for my birthday. We had just returned from Ireland where we fell in love with their fresh scones, so Chuck decided to try making them himself. Our new kitchen was just the spot to try his baking challenge—it was a sweet way to introduce our new kitchen.

—Connie Grazanka

MOLASSES-GRILLED RIB EYE STEAKS

*A new use for an
early American staple.*

1/2 cup	molasses
1/4 cup	coarse-grain Dijon mustard
1 tbs	olive oil
4	(8 to 10 oz) boneless beef rib eye steaks
3/4 tsp	salt
3/4 tsp	pepper

1. Combine molasses, mustard, and olive oil in a shallow dish or large zip top plastic freezer bag.
2. Add steaks, cover and seal, chill at least 2 hours, turning occasionally.
3. Remove steaks and discard marinade.
4. Sprinkle evenly with salt and pepper.
5. Grill covered over medium high heat 5 to 7 minutes on each side or to desired degree of doneness.

THOUGHTS ABOUT
WORKING WITH A
KITCHEN DESIGNER…
*It had become
painfully clear that
we needed an expert
to find the layout
possibilities within the
confines of the
available space. We
were stuck in the early
design phase and
didn't know how to
complete our vision.
Experienced feedback
was needed for all the
ideas we had been
considering.*

—Laura Steele

Recipe provided by Jane VonVoigtlander

A one-dish feast. The Portuguese celebrate their heritage with this hearty meal.

12 lb	chuck roast (without bones), fat removed
2	soup bones for flavor (from butcher)
2 tbs	salt
1 tbs	pepper
1 cup	rosé wine
1/2 cup	pickling spice
1/2 cup	chopped dry onions
2 tbs	celery salt
2 tbs	ground cumin
1 tbs	Worcestershire sauce
1 tbs	garlic puree
3 8 oz	cans tomato sauce
2 large	cabbage heads
4 sprigs	fresh mint
2	loaves French bread
1/2 cup	fresh parsley, chopped

1. Place meat and bones in a 12 quart kettle.
2. Add salt, pepper, wine, and water to cover about 1" above meat and marinate for 5 hours.
3. Wrap pickling spices in cheesecloth, and add to meat.
4. Cook on high heat for 2 hours or until meat easily pulls away from bone.
5. Add remaining ingredients (except cabbage and mint).
6. Bring to boil, then simmer for 30 minutes.
7. Place quartered cabbage on top of meat and continue simmering until cabbage is tender.
8. Remove pickling spices and dispose.
9. Remove meat and cabbage from liquid.
10. Check remaining liquid for texture and taste; add water or salt as necessary.
11. Pour meat and liquid over sliced French bread and top with parsley.

Note: Serves 12

Recipe provided by Jason Siegel
His grandmother's recipe

FAVORITE KITCHEN
ELEMENTS...
    I love the entire layout! The ease of having dishes, silverware, and glasses in the area close to the table. The work area of stove, ovens, and refrigeration make it easy to prepare food and bake.

—Pat Summers

Dessert
THE FINISHING TOUCH

The Brits refer to them as "afters," but we call them necessities.

Richly sweet, or lightly flavorful, fine desserts give everyone

a reason to linger at the table.

GIANT CHOCOLATE TOFFEE COOKIES

APPLE DRIED CHERRY BARS

HEALTHY OATMEAL COOKIES

CHERRY DOROTHY

MAPLE SYRUP COOKIES

APPLE CREAM DESSERT

PISTACHIO PUDDING CAKE

FRESH APPLE CAKE

PUMPKIN PIE DESSERT

BANANA CAKE

YUMMY BARS

DOUBLE TREAT BROWNIES

So good, they deserve to be twice the size.

1/2 cup	all-purpose flour
1 tsp	baking powder
1/4 tsp	salt
1 lb	bittersweet or semisweet chocolate, chopped (not unsweetened)
1/4 cup	unsalted butter
1 3/4 cup	brown sugar, packed
4	large eggs
1 tbs	vanilla extract
4 1.4 oz	chocolate-covered English toffee bars (such as Heath), coarsely chopped
1 cup	pecans, chopped and toasted
	parchment paper

1. Combine flour, baking powder, and salt in small bowl; set aside.
2. Stir chocolate and butter in top of double boiler set over simmering water until melted and smooth.
3. Remove mixture and cool to lukewarm.
4. Using electric mixer, beat sugar and eggs in bowl until thick – about 5 minutes.
5. Beat in chocolate mixture and vanilla.
6. Stir in flour mixture, then toffee and nuts. Batter will be thick.
7. Chill batter until firm – about 45 minutes.
8. Preheat oven to 350°.
9. Line 2 large baking sheets with parchment paper.
10. Scoop batter with 1/4 cup onto sheets, spacing 2 1/2" apart.
11. Bake just until tops are dry and cracked, but cookies are still soft to touch – about 15 minutes.
12. Cool on sheets.

Note: Don't be alarmed: batter will be dense once chilled.
Can be made 2 days ahead. Store in airtight container at room temperature.

FONDEST KITCHEN
MEMORIES…
*Seeing my kids getting
interested in cooking
and having the place
to do it.*

—Tina Griffin

Recipe provided by Pam Johnson

Dried cherries, a northern Michigan favorite,
are reminiscent of raisins, but with a delicate sweetness.

DOUGH

2 1/4 cup	flour
1/2 tsp	salt
1/2 lb	butter, chilled and diced
1/2 cup	water, ice cold

APPLES

12	Granny Smith apples, peeled and sliced
3/4 cup	brown sugar
1 tbs	cinnamon
1 pinch	nutmeg

CREAM

1 cup	plus 2 tbs sugar
1/2 cup	flour
1/2 tsp	salt
2 1/2 tsp	vanilla
2 cup	heavy cream

STREUSEL

3 cups	flour
1 1/2 cup	brown sugar
3/4 tsp	cinnamon
3/4 lb	butter
1 cup	dried cherries

Recipe provided by Karen Williams
Galley Gourmet

PIE DOUGH

1. Place flour and salt in a mixing bowl; cut in diced butter.
2. Working quickly with the hands, rub flour into the butter, stopping when butter pieces resemble the size of walnuts.
3. Add cold water all at once to flour/butter mixture.
4. Stir until just combined. (There should still be visible lumps of butter.)
5. Cover dough with plastic wrap and refrigerator at least 8 hours.
6. Remove dough from refrigerator until room temperature and workable.
7. Flour cutting board and roll out dough to 13"x18" rectangle.
8. Coat 13"x18" jellyroll pan with non-stick spray and parchment paper.
9. Place dough rectangle inside pan and prick it lightly with fork.
10. Refrigerate until needed.
11. Preheat oven to 375°.

FILLINGS

1. Toss apples with brown sugar, cinnamon, and nutmeg; set aside.
2. Combine all ingredients for cream into bowl and stir; set aside.

STREUSEL

1. Combine flour, brown sugar, and cinnamon in mixing bowl.
2. Cut butter into dice and work into flour mixture by hand.

ASSEMBLY

1. Distribute dried cherries over pie dough.
2. Pour cream mixture over dried cherries and mound apples on top. (Apples will cook down later.)
3. Sprinkle streusel topping over apples.
4. Place in oven and bake for about 45 minutes, until apples are bubbling and the streusel is golden brown.
5. Allow to cool completely before cutting into 3"x3" squares.

FAVORITE KITCHEN
FEATURE...
Cooler and veggie
drawers—used ALL
the time.

—Susie Simon

HEALTHY OATMEAL COOKIES

Yes, you could even have them for breakfast.

I cup	"Smart Balance" or non-trans-fat butter
I cup	sugar or Splenda
2	eggs or Egg Beaters
5 tbs	skim milk
I tsp	vanilla
dash	salt
2 cups	oatmeal (not quick oats)
I cup	whole wheat flour
I cup	white or bran flour (can use 2 cups whole wheat flour instead for heavier cookie)
3/4 tsp	baking soda
I I/2 tsp	cinnamon
I cup	dried cherries or raisins
	nuts or mini chocolate chips, optional

1. Preheat oven to 350°.

2. Cream butter and sugar.

3. Add egg, milk, vanilla, and dash of salt in medium bowl.

4. Mix dry ingredients in large bowl.

5. Add egg mixture to dry ingredients.

6. Mix thoroughly.

7. Drop by spoonful onto cookie sheet sprayed with vegetable oil.

8. Bake for 10 to15 minutes.

Note: Disguised oatmeal cookies have been a favorite at my house. Kids never had a clue that they were eating a low-fat, low-sugar cookie. They made this nurse very happy that I could give them a healthier cookie.

THOUGHTS ABOUT
WORKING WITH A
KITCHEN DESIGNER…
It is a must. The knowledge and experience that Liz has is worth its weight in gold.

—John & Nancy Banks

Recipe provided by Michele Sturt
Adapted from 1983 Mom and Me cookbook
Revised by a mom with nutrition in mind.

No relation to
Apple Brown Betty.

1	large can cherry pie filling
1	package white cake mix
1/2 cup	stick of butter
3/4 cup	walnuts, chopped
	coconut to taste

1. Preheat oven to 325°.

2. Butter 9"×13" glass baking dish.

3. Spread cherries across dish. Sprinkle cake mix over cherries.

4. Melt butter and drizzle over cake mix.

5. Top with chopped walnuts and coconut.

6. Bake until brown.

Recipe provided by Libby Follis
Mom's recipe

KITCHEN DREAMS
AND GOALS…
We wanted a small,
cozy, but very
functional kitchen
for preparing dinner
for two, or twenty,
or more.

—Susie Simon

MAPLE SYRUP COOKIES

Try these with ice cream.

1 1/2 cup	sugar
1 cup	butter, softened
2 cups	flour
1	egg yolk
2	eggs
1/2 cup	real maple syrup
1 1/2 cup	pecans, coarsely chopped

1. Preheat oven to 350°.

2. Butter 9"x15" pan.

3. Mix 1 cup sugar and butter in bowl until creamy.

4 Add flour and mix.

5. Stir in yolk and mix.

6. Turn dough into pan and pat evenly over bottom.

7. Set aside.

8. Put 2 eggs in bowl and beat until foamy.

9. Add remaining 1/2 cup sugar and syrup; beat 1 minute.

10. Pour egg mixture over dough.

11. Sprinkle pecans on top.

12. Bake 40 to 45 minutes.

13. Cut into 1 1/2" squares while warm, and cool in pan.

Note: Cookies should look caramel-colored and soft to the touch, but not sticky. They'll become firm when cool.

THOUGHTS ABOUT
WORKING WITH A
KITCHEN DESIGNER…
*It was great
having a designer
to explain all the
elements to us.*

—Dana Selis

Recipe provided by Laura Steele

As American as apple pie,
only different.

CRUST

2 cups	flour
3 tbs	sugar
I cup	margarine

FILLING

4	large Granny Smith apples, thinly sliced
I cup	sugar
3 tsp	cinnamon
3	small or 2 large packages vanilla pudding (not instant)
2	small cartons whipping cream

1. Preheat oven to 350°.

2. Blend flour, sugar, and margarine.

3. Press into bottom of 10"×15" jelly roll pan.

4. Pare and slice apples (about 1/2" thick), and arrange neatly in one layer over crust.

5. Mix together sugar and cinnamon.

6. Sprinkle over apple slices.

7. Bake for 30 minutes.

8. Cover with foil, and then bake 15 minutes more.

9. Prepare pudding according to pie directions on the pudding box.

10. Pour hot pudding over cooked apples.

11. Chill.

12. Top with sweetened whipped cream.

Note: Can be made a day ahead.

Serves up to 16.

Recipe provided by Cathy Scriven
Mom's recipe

FONDEST KITCHEN
MEMORY...
For us, it's all about
the kitchen. The
kitchen is where our
life comes alive.

—Margy Kidd

This Middle Eastern nut was a favorite snack of the Queen of Sheba.

CAKE

	I	box white cake mix
I cup		oil
	3	eggs
	I	package instant pistachio pudding mix
I cup		club soda
I cup		pistachio nuts

ICING

	I	small carton Cool Whip (2 cups)
I cup		milk
	I	package instant pistachio pudding mix

CAKE

1. Preheat oven to 350°.
2. Mix all cake ingredients in order listed.
3. Bake in a greased tube pan for 45 minutes.
4. Cool.

ICING

1. Whip icing ingredients with hand mixer.
2. Ice cake after cooled.

THOUGHTS ABOUT
WORKING WITH A
KITCHEN DESIGNER...
As I am an interior designer, I appreciate a kitchen designer who is familiar with the specific challenges and products for the kitchen.

—Glenda Jehle

Recipe provided by Diane Brooks
Mom's Recipe

Straight from the orchard.

APPLE MIXTURE

3 cups	Granny Smith apples, chopped
2 tsp	lemon juice
2 tbs	cinnamon

CAKE

2 cups	sugar
1 1/2 cup	oil
2	eggs
3 cups	flour
1/2 tsp	salt
1 cup	pecans or walnuts, chopped
1/2 tsp	nutmeg
1/2 tsp	mace
1 tsp	baking soda
2 tsp	vanilla

ICING

4 oz	package cream cheese
1 cup	powdered sugar
1/2 cup	butter, room temperature

CAKE

1. Preheat oven to 325°.
2. In a mixing bowl, sprinkle chopped apples with lemon juice and cinnamon. Set aside.
3. Combine cake ingredients together until well blended. Add apple mixture.
4. Pour into greased 9"x13" or bundt cake pan.
5. For 9"x13", bake for 60 minutes; for bundt pan, bake for 90 minutes.

ICING

1. Combine cream cheese, powdered sugar, and butter.
2. Spread on cooled cake.

Note: Double icing recipe for extra frosting.

Recipe provided by Sue Hartemayer
From friend, Jane Walling

PUMPKIN PIE DESSERT

A holiday favorite,
all dressed up.

1 29 oz	can pumpkin filling
1 cup	sugar
1 tsp	cinnamon
1/2 tsp	salt
1/2 tsp	nutmeg
1/2 tsp	ginger
4	eggs, beaten
12 oz	can evaporated milk
1	package yellow cake mix (2-layer size)
1 cup	nuts, chopped
3/4 cup	melted butter
	whipped cream, optional

1. Preheat oven to 350°.
2. Combine pumpkin, sugar, cinnamon, salt, nutmeg, and ginger.
3. Add eggs.
4. Beat lightly with wooden spoon until combined.
5. Gradually stir in evaporated milk; mix well.
6. Pour into greased 9"x13" baking dish.
7. Sprinkle with cake mix and nuts.
8. Drizzle with melted butter.
9. Bake 50 minutes or until edges are firm and top is golden brown.
10. Cool in pan.
11. Cover and chill at least 2 hours before serving.
12. Served with sweetened whipped cream.

KITCHEN DESIGN
DREAMS AND GOALS…
The design keeps the
non-participants out of
the way of the cook.
And even more
important, the cook
(usually me) gets the
vantage point of
seeing all the lake
activity, living room,
family room, patio and
porch areas, and front
entry. How good
is that?

—Linda Johnson

Recipe provided by Sue Glover

Could count as a fruit
on the food pyramid.

1/3 cup	butter, softened
1 cup	sugar
1	egg
3	ripe bananas, mashed
1 3/4 cup	flour
1 1/2 tsp	baking soda dissolved in a little milk or cream

1. Preheat oven to 350°.

2. Mix butter, sugar, egg, and bananas.

3. Add the flour and baking soda.

4. Bake in a buttered, 8" or 9" round cake pan for 30 to 35 minutes or until toothpick inserted in center comes out clean.

Note: Double recipe for 9"x13" pan and bake for approximately 45 minutes. This is a great recipe and much easier to make than banana bread.

THOUGHTS ABOUT
WORKING WITH A
KITCHEN DESIGNER...
It is a tremendous help
to have a layout that
takes advantage of the
space you have
available.

—Pat Summers

Recipe provided by Debbie Nactrab

YUMMY BARS

Need we say more?

3 tbs	butter or margarine
16 oz	miniature marshmallows
1/2 cup	peanut butter
1/2 cup	peanuts
1/2 cup	almonds
1 cup	granola (plain)
1 cup	semisweet chocolate chips
2 cups	Total cereal
2 cups	Cheerios

1. Melt butter and marshmallows in covered pan.
2. Stir in peanut butter.
3. Add peanuts, almonds, and granola.
4. Stir to coat thoroughly.
5. Remove pan from stove.
6. Fold in chocolate chips and cereals.
7. Press mixture into 9"x13" pan coated with non-stick spray.
8. Let cool, then cut into squares and serve.

KITCHEN DESIGN
DREAMS AND GOALS...
*To create a space
that was colorful,
warm, and looked
like it had always
been part of our
vacation home.*

—Kathleen &
Larry Acker

Recipe provided by Holli Banks

DOUBLE TREAT BROWNIES

Chocolate[2]

4 oz	unsweetened chocolate (4 squares)
1 cup	butter or margarine, softened to room temperature
2 cups	sugar
4	eggs
1 1/2 tsp	vanilla
1 cup	flour
1 1/2 cup	chopped nuts, divided
1 cup	semisweet chocolate chips (6 oz package)

1. Preheat oven to 350°.
2. In top of double boiler over simmering (not boiling) water, melt chocolate; cool.
3. Grease and flour 9"x13" baking pan.
4. In a large bowl, cream butter or margarine.
5. Gradually add sugar to butter and continue beating until light and fluffy.
6. Beat in eggs, one at a time, until well combined.
7. Beat in melted chocolate and vanilla.
8. Beat in flour just until combined.
9. Stir in 1 cup nuts and chocolate chips.
10. Spread evenly into prepared pan.
11. Sprinkle with remaining 1/2 cup nuts.
12. Bake for 30 to 35 minutes or until a cake tester inserted in center comes out clean.
13. Cover until cool.
14. Chill.
15. Cut into bars. Store in airtight container.

Makes about 30 brownies

Recipe provided by Sandy Kasischke
Adapted from Detroit Free Press
recipe (1970's)

THOUGHTS ON
WORKING WITH A
KITCHEN DESIGNER...
A builder's home
is a reflection of his
business. I wanted the
best design integrated
with the best kitchen
products. Liz brought
those traits to
my business and
to my home.

—Dan Sebold

Sources

DESIGN DETAILS

The companies listed below are well-represented in this book, and their products are considered among the best on the market. Use this guide to find the same products for your own kitchen project.

DUTCH MADE CABINETRY
260-657-3311 · www.dutchmade.com
Crafting handmade custom cabinetry since 1967.

TREVARROW
800-482-1948
A wholesale distributor of residential kitchen equipment, specializing in upscale, built in products for the home.

DIXIE CUT STONE & MARBLE, INC.
888-450-1890 · www.dixiestone.com
Michigan's largest supplier of natural and man-made stone products.

GINIVITO TILE & STONE
231-439-9764 · 231-348-8229
Providing unparalleled design and installation to enhance the beauty of your home; we leave no stone unturned.

NORTHERN MICHIGAN CUT STONE
231-439-0500 · www.northernmichigancutstone.com
Specializing in granite, marble, limestone, and concrete countertops.

MICHIGAN MAPLE BLOCK CO.
231-347-4170 · www.mapleblock.com
125 years making the world's finest butcher block.

Acknowledgements

A COMPENDIUM OF SOURCES

The following architects, builders, interior designers, photographers, and stylists

played an integral part in the creation of the kitchens within this book

and the photography that showcases them.

ARCHED TO PERFECTION — PAGE 10, 44

ARCHITECT	Alexander V. Bogaerts & Associates
BUILDER	Thomas Sebold & Associates Inc
INTERIOR DESIGNER	Caryn Satovsky-Siegel, Alexander V. Bogaerts & Associates
PHOTOGRAPHER	Beth Singer
STYLIST	Annie Kleene

THE NATURAL — PAGE 48

ARCHITECT	Ike Kligerman Barkley Architects
BUILDER	Thomas Sebold & Associates Inc
INTERIOR DESIGNER	Ike Kligerman Barkley Architects
PHOTOGRAPHER	Tom Galliher Photography
STYLIST	Alan Nauts

CONTEMPORARY ELEGANCE — PAGE 12, 36, 52

ARCHITECT	Rugo Raff Limited Architects
BUILDER	Evening Star Joinery
INTERIOR DESIGNER	Thomas Stringer Inc.
PHOTOGRAPHER	Steve Vorderman Photography
STYLIST	Alan Nauts

CLASSICALLY INSPIRED — PAGE 56

ARCHITECT	Nicholas White, AIA, N.J. White Associates Architecture & Planning,
BUILDER	Thomas Sebold & Associates Inc
INTERIOR DESIGNER	Marty Walstrom, Great Lakes Design
PHOTOGRAPHER	James Yochum Photography
STYLIST	Gisela Rose

AT THE COTTAGE — PAGE 60

BUILDER	Kane Construction
INTERIOR DESIGNER	Patricia Wood & Co.
PHOTOGRAPHER	Steve Vorderman Photography
STYLIST	Alan Nauts

SEEING RED — PAGE 34, 64

ARCHITECT	Tom Borger, Borger Associates
BUILDER	Matthews Construction
INTERIOR DESIGNER	Pam Beam
PHOTOGRAPHER	David Duncan Livingston

TONE ON TONE — PAGE 68

ARCHITECT	James D. Nordlie, AIA, Archiventure Group Architects
BUILDER	Thomas Sebold & Associates Inc
INTERIOR DESIGNER	Jim Dutkowski
PHOTOGRAPHER	David Duncan Livingston
STYLIST	David Duncan Livingston

MIXED METALS ARE A STANDOUT — PAGE 70

BUILDER	Behan Construction
INTERIOR DESIGNER	Contract Interiors
PHOTOGRAPHER	David Duncan Livingston
STYLIST	David Duncan Livingston

UP AT THE CABIN — PAGE 30, 72

BUILDER	Gale Charbonneau, Bay Area Maintenance & Construction
PHOTOGRAPHER	David Duncan Livingston
STYLIST	David Duncan Livingston

DESIGN AT WORK — PAGE 8, 74

ARCHITECT	Nicholas White, AIA N.J White Associates Architecture & Planning
BUILDER	David McBride, McBride Construction Inc
PHOTOGRAPHER	Steve Vorderman Photography
STYLIST	Alan Nauts

THE WEEKENDER — PAGE 76

ARCHITECT	DesRosiers Architects Inc
BUILDER	Kane Construction
INTERIOR DESIGNER	Patricia Wood & Co.
PHOTOGRAPHER	Tom Galliher Photography
STYLIST	Alan Nauts

OLD ENGLISH WARMTH — PAGE 80

ARCHITECT	Nicholas White, AIA
	N.J White Associates Architecture & Planning
BUILDER	Birchwood Construction
INTERIOR DESIGNER	Kennedy & Co.
PHOTOGRAPHER	Steve Vorderman Photography
STYLIST	Alan Nauts

A TASTE OF PROVENCE — PAGE 82

BUILDER	Doug DeRocher
PHOTOGRAPHER	Steve Vorderman Photography
STYLIST	Alan Nauts

DESIGN FOR LIVING — PAGE 84

ARCHITECT	Todd Young, AIA, Young & Young Architects Inc.
BUILDER	Thomas Sebold & Associates Inc
INTERIOR DESIGNER	Noni Pace-Morgridge, Pace Interior Design
PHOTOGRAPHER	Tom Galliher Photography
STYLIST	Alan Nauts

WITH GRAND DESIGNS — PAGE 86

ARCHITECT	Alexander V. Bogaerts & Associates
BUILDER	Thomas Sebold & Associates Inc
INTERIOR DESIGNER	Caryn Satovsky-Siegel, Alexander V. Bogaerts & Associates
PHOTOGRAPHER	Tom Galliher Photography
STYLIST	Alan Nauts

CRAFTSMAN SPIRIT — PAGE 88

| PHOTOGRAPHER | David Duncan Livingston |
| STYLIST | David Duncan Livingston |

AN ISLAND FOR GATHERING — PAGE 90

ARCHITECT	James D. Nordlie, AIA, Archiventure Group Associates
BUILDER	Thomas Sebold & Associates Inc
INTERIOR DESIGNER	Kennedy & Co.
PHOTOGRAPHER	John Wooden Photography

ROOM TO MOVE — PAGE 92

BUILDER	Chamberlain Building & Remodeling
INTERIOR DESIGNER	Laurie Seltenright, L.S Design
PHOTOGRAPHER	James Yochum Photography
STYLIST	Gisela Rose

OLD WORLD INFLUENCE — PAGE 94

ARCHITECT	Todd Young, AIA, Young & Young Architects Inc.
BUILDER	Thomas Sebold & Associates Inc
PHOTOGRAPHER	Tom Galliher Photography
STYLIST	Alan Nauts

TRIANGLE IN THE ROUND — PAGE 96

ARCHITECT	Douglas A. Wright Architect
BUILDER	Bill Noblett, Carpentree Inc.
PHOTOGRAPHER	Tom Galliher Photography
STYLIST	Alan Nauts

LET THERE BE LIGHT — PAGE 98

ARCHITECT	Alexander V. Bogaerts & Associates
BUILDER	Templeton Building Company
INTERIOR DESIGNER	Caryn Satovsky-Seigal, Alexander V. Bogaerts & Associates
PHOTOGRAPHER	Steve Vorderman Photography
STYLIST	Annie Kleene

FARMHOUSE REVISITED — PAGE 102

ARCHITECT	Jodi Alger Lyons, Home Planning & Design, Ltd.
BUILDER	Northwinds Custom Homes
PHOTOGRAPHER	Steve Vorderman Photography
STYLIST	Alan Nauts

TO THE MANOR BORN — PAGE 104

ARCHITECT	William Baldner, AIA
	Clifford N. Wright Associates Architects
BUILDER	Brian Haase, owner, Earl Ristow Wood Products
INTERIOR DESIGNER	Daniel Clancey, Perlmutter & Freiwald
PHOTOGRAPHER	Steve Vorderman Photography
STYLIST	Alan Nauts

SPECIAL THANK YOU

PHILIP SHIPPERT, SHIPPERT PHOTOGRAPHY — FOOD PHOTOGRAPHER

LAURA GOBLE — FOOD PHOTOGRAPHY STYLIST

CAROL SCHALLA, MIDWEST LIVING®

CHUCKS APPLIANCES — PHOTOGRAPHY PROPS

CIAO BELLA! GARDEN & HOME — PHOTOGRAPHY PROPS

LOST & FOUND ANTIQUES — PHOTOGRAPHY PROPS

NORTHERN MICHIGAN CUT STONE — PHOTOGRAPHY PROPS

RUSSELL HARDWARE — PHOTOGRAPHY PROPS

CAMERON VAN DYKE, LLC   LIGHTING DESIGNER

MIKE GULLON, PHOENIX PHOTOGRAPHY

GRIBI BUILDERS

HERITAGE CUSTOM KITCHENS

M.L. FOWLER & CO.

PHOTO CREDIT

PAGE 31 — STAINLESS THREE-BOWL SINK — PHOTOGRAPHY COURTESY OF *MIDWEST LIVING®* MAGAZINE; PHOTOGRAPHER: GORDON BEALL.

Cooking Lessons

LIZ AND HER DAD, CIRCA 1962.
STORM LAKE, IOWA.
THIS WAS BUT A SMALL INDICATION
OF BIGGER THINGS TO COME.